How to Write and Sell
Romance Novels

How to Write & Sell
Romance Novels

A Step-by-Step Guide

Linda Lee

HEARTSONG PRESS
Edmonds, Washington

Copyright ©1988 by Linda Lee
Heartsong Press, P.O. Box 238
Edmonds, WA 98020
First Edition: July, 1988
   3 4 5 6 7 8 9 10

Cover Design: Martine Richards
Typography: Technigraphic Systems, Inc. • Edmonds, WA
Printing: BookCrafters, Michigan

Cataloging Data

Lee, Linda
   How to write and sell romance novels; a step-by-step guide.
   Bibliography.
   Includes index.
   1. Love stories—Authorship. I. Title.
1988 808.3'85
Library of Congress Catalog Card Number: 88-81232
ISBN 0-929195-00-0

This book may be ordered directly from the publisher.
Heartsong Press, P.O. Box 238, Edmonds, WA 98020.
Please include $9.95 plus $1.50 postage and handling for the first book
and $.50 for each additional book ordered. Washington residents please
add $.78 for tax.

Printed in the United States of America

To my sister, Rosemary, who suggested I write this book.

And to the members of my Romance Writing Workshop, for whom these lessons were originally created.

Contents

Introduction

*T*he fiction marketplace is made up of two kinds of books: mainstream and genre, or category fiction. Mainstream stories are aimed at a broad variety of readers, while genre books are for people who favor particular types of stories, such as westerns, mysteries, science fiction, occult, or romances. A mainstream story can include these elements, but they will be part of a greater whole. In a mainstream novel, the theme, plot, and characters often are more complex than those encountered in genre fiction. In a genre novel, the plot follows a specific formula, and characters are conceived and developed to fit the established pattern. The story is told primarily through action and dialogue, with a minimum of character introspection.

This does not mean that genre fiction is easier to write than mainstream fiction. Nor does it mean that the writer should approach the task without sincerity and a desire to tell the best possible story. Readers are quick to spot a writer who does not share their enthusiasm or respect for the genre. Also, it does not mean that the writer cannot be creative or original. Like musical compositions, the formulas allow for variations on a theme, and the best way to capture a reader's attention is to come up with a story that, while it fits the formula's parameters, still offers something different. It is this challenge that makes genre writing worthy of the writer's efforts.

Of all the categories, the romance is probably the most popular. The romance has been around for a long time, in one form or another. The word romance originally meant a language derived from Latin or "Roman," such as French, Spanish, or Italian. Later, the term was applied to tales told by troubadours, the traveling poet-musicians of the twelfth and thirteenth centuries. Since most of these stories were of knights and their heroic deeds, the word romance came to mean stories that were larger than life, stories often based on legend or on the supernatural.

Many of these tales included what was known as courtly love. Courtly love described the relationship between a knight and a woman of higher station, usually a woman attached to the royal court. People believed that this kind of love was true love and that it was impossible to attain in a marriage. The lovers carried on an illicit, secret relationship, pledging to remain faithful despite all obstacles. Courtly love was accompanied by such emotional disturbances as loss of appetite, pallor, and sleeplessness.

This idea of a true love became known as romantic love and through the ages continued to be expressed in novels such as Samuel Richardson's *Pamela*, Charlotte Bronte's *Jane Eyre*, and Daphne Du Maurier's *Rebecca*.

Today, scholars still define romances as stories that deal with the remote in time or place, with the heroic, the adventurous, the mysterious. Stories that are, in effect, larger than life.

The popular definition of romance fiction, the one that we are concerned with, affirms that while these stories may have elements of fantasy, they are grounded in reality. They deal with real people in real situations. As romances, they focus on the development of a love relationship between a man and a woman. Two people meet, fall in love, encounter obstacles to the fulfillment of their love, eventually conquer those obstacles, and live happily ever after. The basic message is: Love conquers all.

While today's romantic love still is idealistic, in that it is the perfect, true, and lasting love, it is, after all obstacles have been overcome, attainable in marriage. The reader knows that in the end the hero and heroine will marry and that their union will last forever. The enjoyable part is finding out exactly how it all comes about.

This book will show you how to construct a romance, from idea to finished manuscript, and how to get it published. Part I includes what you need to know and do before you begin to write. You'll learn the formula requirements and how to develop interesting, believable characters and exciting, workable plots. Part II gives the techniques you'll need as you write the story, techniques for establishing sexual tension and conflict and for writing snappy dialogue and sensuous love scenes. Part III instructs you on marketing your manuscript, how to find an agent or how to do it on your own.

As you use this book, keep two things in mind: 1) You do not have to work sequentially through the chapters. Every writer works differently. Start where the book will help you the most. 2) I've tried to make the information as generic as possible; however, a changing market is inevitable. Read the romances currently being published. Write to the editors for guidelines. Then adapt what you find here to meet the new rules.

PART I

Laying the Groundwork

CHAPTER 1
Understanding the Formula

*A*man and a woman meet, fall in love, encounter obstacles to their love, overcome the obstacles, marry, and live happily ever after. You've seen that happen in any number of books, books that aren't necessarily category fiction. When this formula is applied to genre romances, it includes some specific requirements. The characters have certain restrictions regarding age, personality type, and appearance. The plot develops along certain lines. Before you begin to write your novel, you should be aware of these formula demands.

CHARACTER REQUIREMENTS

THE HEROINE

Age. Romantic heroines range in age from nineteen to forty. The most frequently used ages are between twenty-five and thirty-five.

Maturity. No matter what her age, she is mature in attitude and behavior. Gone are the silly, impulsive young women who populated the pages of earlier category romances. Oh, she may have some immature quirk or habit that gets her into trouble, but, overall, she acts like an adult.

Independence. Along with maturity goes an ability to make her own way. She is not looking for a man to provide her livelihood; rather, she has either her own career or another source of income. If she does not have a profession, she has a strong interest in something worthwhile.

Appearance. She is attractive, but her appearance need not be perfect. Often a slight physical flaw—perhaps her feet are too big or her nose too long—makes her more believable and easier for the reader to identify with. However, she never has a disfigurement that might be found repulsive.

Romantic vulnerability. Despite her maturity and independence, when it comes to love she is vulnerable. Whether she admits it or not, she is looking for that one true and lasting love, and matters of the heart often overrule considerations of the head.

THE HERO

Age. His age range is from late twenties to mid-forties. While he usually is older than the heroine, the gap must not be a May-December one.

Appearance. Like the heroine, he is attractive, but his physical appearance need not be flawless. His features and build should suggest virility, strength, and power rather than mirror a classic handsomeness.

Temperament. He is masterful and aggressive, but on appropriate occasions he also can be tender, sensitive, and caring. He must be able to respond emotionally to the heroine.

Livelihood. He, too, usually has a profession in which he is successful. If he is not yet established, he has the capacity to succeed. He is a winner, never a loser.

SECONDARY CHARACTERS

Secondary characters fulfill definite purposes. Often they are confidants to the heroine and the hero. The heroine's confidant may be a woman her own age or an older person, perhaps an aunt or an uncle. The hero's confidant may be a coworker or a childhood friend.

Secondary characters often are the means by which the main characters meet. They may provide plot complications as the story goes along, and at the end help the lovers achieve the come-to-realize that brings about their final union.

In longer stories, secondary characters may provide the subplot. The subplot is another, not as fully developed, story that runs concurrently with the main plot. Like the main characters, secondary characters have problems to solve or goals to reach, encounter obstacles, and at the end either do or do not attain their objectives.

However, despite the story's length, all romances focus on the interaction between the hero and the heroine; therefore, both the number and the development of secondary characters are minimal.

PLOT REQUIREMENTS

1. The plot is set in motion when a main character, usually the heroine, takes action to solve a problem, reach a goal, or fulfill a need.

2. She may meet the hero for the first time during the course of the story, or she may have known him earlier.

3. The lovers-to-be should interact as soon as possible after the story begins. If they don't get together in the first chapter, one or the other is foreshadowed; that is, introduced to us in conversation or in the thoughts of another character.

4. When the hero and heroine do meet, two things invariably happen: They are physically attracted to each other and at the same time repelled by some conflict. This establishes the sexual tension that will prevail throughout the story.

5. The plot has two parts: what happens as the heroine tries to solve her problem and what happens in her relationship with the hero. The development of their relationship receives the most emphasis. Note: It is possible to write a successful romance without a goal for the heroine, but if this if your first attempt, I recommend constructing the two plot lines. Often, the personal goal plot can provide a framework for the love affair.

6. The story is told primarily through action and dialogue, with a minimum of narration.

7. The love relationship includes sexual intercourse (known in the trade as a "sensuous" romance), or it does not (a "sweet" romance). The degree of physical intimacy depends either on your choice or on the requirements of the line you are aiming for.

8. Near the end, the story has a "black period," when the lovers are separated and it looks as though their love is doomed.

9. The lovers finally resolve all their conflicts and the story ends with their marriage in the offing.

10. Although specific dates are not given, the stories take place in the present.

11. The plot may contain elements of mystery or suspense, but in a pure romance the mystery never overshadows the love affair. Stories that have equal parts romance and mystery usually are called romantic suspense stories.

12. Most lines have some plot taboos. Generally, such social problems as abortion, drug addiction, spouse abuse, criminal behavior, and mental illness are not acceptable backdrops. These subjects tend to detract from a romantic atmosphere. Politics, particularly terrorism and kidnapping, is also a touchy area. The best plots are built around personal problems of the main characters rather than around issues that affect the fate of the world.

TO DO:

Read a variety of romance novels. Analyze them by answering these questions:

1. What are the ages of the main characters?

2. What are their occupations or special interests?

3. What is the goal/problem/need of each?

4. How soon after the story opens do they interact?

5. What is the conflict between the two?

6. Is their love consummated? If so, how far into the story does it occur? How many such love scenes are there?

7. Who are the secondary characters? What are their functions?

CHAPTER 2
Getting Ideas

*W*ith the formula and its requirements in mind, begin to develop your story. You can start with an idea and create characters to fit that idea, or you can begin with the characters and let them determine the story. If you prefer to begin with a character, you may want to skip ahead to Chapter 3. However, be sure you return to this chapter at some point, as it contains important information about other aspects of the story.

Here are some approaches that may help you get your story started:

A SETTING

Your story may be set anywhere in the world. Certain places—an island in the Caribbean, a village in Italy, a castle in England—seem made for romance. But suppose you haven't been to any exotic locations? Many authors have written romances set in places they haven't visited. Careful and thorough research can supply all the information you need. Besides books and magazines, use travel brochures, road maps and atlases, slides and photos, video tapes, TV and movie travelogues. Pay particular attention to such things as flora and fauna, habits and customs, and the weather. These details, when subtly woven into the story, give the reader a you-are-there feeling.

However, your setting need not be unusual or far removed from your own backyard. With proper treatment even the most ordinary locations can be made to appear romantic. I'll discuss specifically how to do this in Chapter 6, but, briefly, here's the trick: show how your characters respond sensuously to their environment. How does a cool breeze make your heroine feel? The sun on a hot day? The sounds of traffic in the city or of animals in the woods nearby? The smell of dinner cooking on the stove or of the flowers sent by her lover? The taste of wine? The touch of silk? These kinds of sensuous observations can turn the most mundane setting into a romantic paradise.

A CAREER

Here, also, the field is wide open. Perhaps you can use your own profession or that of someone you know. A career that carries an aura of glamour, such as modeling, fashion designing, or cosmetics, is a plus.

9

Choose carefully, however, as many professions have been overused. Your best bet is to search out new and unusual interests for your characters. Again, it will be your *treatment* of the subject that will provide the romance.

As with the setting, if you choose an unfamiliar career, research it thoroughly. High school and college libraries are good sources of career and occupational information.

A PERSONAL EXPERIENCE

Particularly if you are a beginning writer, you may find it easier to write about something you have experienced rather than to write from imagination. There's nothing wrong with that; most fiction has at least some part that came from the real world. Rarely, however, will all of the personal experience work as a drama. Details may have to be altered, events rearranged, and perhaps new characters created. Sometimes, understandably, you are reluctant to tamper with the facts. "But that's not the way it happened!" you protest. Know that your readers do not care how it really happened; if they wanted reality, they would read biographies and other nonfiction. Romance readers are looking for a good story, regardless of its veracity. Therefore, if you wish to use a personal experience, be willing to do what you need to do to make it work dramatically. To be blunt, be willing to lie!

With that in mind, think about your own love relationships. What was your first love like? What did you do? Where did you go? Get in touch with the various feelings—joy, sorrow, anger, passion—that you experienced during the relationship.

A CONFLICT

Conflict is an important part of any story, but it is particularly important in a romance. Since the hero and heroine have fallen in love—even if they do not at first admit it—it is conflict that keeps them apart. You must sustain their conflicts for at least two hundred pages; therefore, you need to choose significant issues.

There are three sources of conflict: 1) man against man, 2) man against himself, and 3) man against nature. Let's see how you can apply these to romance stories.

Man Against Man:

1. The hero and heroine have opposing goals. In my *Yesterday's Promises* (Thomas Bouregy, 1987), Andrea wants to keep the high-rises out of her small home town. Jason is an out-of-town developer who wants to build a condominium. When these two meet, conflict! In my *A Love Song for Lani* (Thomas Bouregy, 1987), Lani is a singer who wants commercial success, and Adam is a musician who will not sacrifice his artistic integrity for money. Conflict!

2. The hero and heroine have opposite character traits. Character traits are aspects of our personality that influence how we behave. Reliability is a trait. Industriousness is a trait. So are laziness, carelessness, and dishonesty. (See Appendix 2 for a list of traits.) Putting together two people with opposite traits results in conflict. In my *The Love Match* (Thomas Bouregy, 1985), Diana is a workaholic, and Alex is a laidback, put-it-off-until-tomorrow type. Can you imagine these two trying to spend a leisurely day together?

3. A situation creates the conflict. In Virginia Myers's *Sunlight on Sand* (Harlequin Superromance, 1984), Janet blames Todd for creating the circumstance that caused the death of her father. In my *Home for the Heart* (Manor Books, 1979), Elaine is suspicious of the mysterious woman in Justin's life. As long as it provides a strong reason for keeping the heroine and hero apart, you can use just about anything. Be creative.

Man Against Himself:

An internal conflict prevents one or the other from making a commitment. Perhaps she finds it impossible to get over the death of her husband. Perhaps he mistrusts all women because a woman in his past was unfaithful. Be careful here, though. At this writing, fear of involvement because of previous unsuccessful relationships is considered cliché.

Man Against Nature:

While this type of conflict obviously won't be between the hero and the heroine, it might be used in other aspects of the story. For example, a character is shipwrecked and must struggle for survival.

Most likely, you will need more than one conflict to sustain even the shortest novel (approximately 50,000 words). A combination I have used is one major conflict and one or two minor ones; for example, opposing goals and opposite traits.

TO DO:

Use one of the above approaches—setting, career, personal experience, conflict—to get an idea for a story. Then do some brainstorming until you have the following:

A setting

A heroine with a profession and a problem/goal/need

A hero with a profession and a problem/goal/need

A conflict between the hero and the heroine

To understand better what I mean, let's work through the process together. We'll begin with a setting. Our story will take place in the mountains where you have a vacation cabin. How could that location be used in a romance? A mountain setting suggests getting away from it all, so let's say the heroine has gone there to be alone. Why would she want to be alone? Maybe to recover from some disaster or disappointment. We'll decide that she's just been overlooked for an important job promotion. What is her job? How about botanist? That might work in later with the mountain setting.

Now we need a hero and a conflict. The conflict could have something to do with the cabin. Suppose the cabin belonged to her uncle and was left to her in his will. However, when she arrives, she finds that a neighbor, who just happens to be a very attractive man, also claims ownership. He says he has proof her uncle didn't own the cabin, and therefore her claim is invalid. He's a geologist who plans to live there while he searches for a legendary lost mine.

We now have a setting, a heroine with a profession and a need, a hero with a profession and a need, and a conflict between the two. Our story is beginning to jell. Now it's time to do some more development of the characters and the plot.

CHAPTER 3
Developing the Characters

*N*o matter where the idea for your story comes from, eventually you must deal with the characters, as it is the characters who will act out the ideas. Before you begin writing, you should know as much as possible about your story people, particularly the heroine and the hero. In fact, it's a good idea to know even more about them than you need to tell their story. The more you know about them, even such seemingly irrelevant facts as their favorite colors and their brands of toothpaste, the more they will come alive on the page.

You have seen how characters in romance novels have built-in requirements. These requirements provide an outline to work from. Now you need to transform these generic people into individuals.

One way to do this is to develop a character biography. This may seem time-consuming, especially if you are eager to get the story under way, but be assured that it will be worth the extra effort. Below is an example of a character biography. It is based on Syd Field's approach in his book *Screenplay* (Dell, 1982). (See Appendix 1 for a reproducible copy.) In each of the chart's sections, you will build on the previous section to create an individual who is different from others of the genre.

CHARACTER BIOGRAPHY

1. *VITAL STATISTICS*

A. Name.

B. Age.

C. Birthdate.

D. Birthplace.

E. Physical description.

To determine age and physical description, draw on the formula requirements. Include height, weight, color of hair and eyes, and any flaws or other distinguishing features. Anything that will make this person stand out from others of similar appearance and age.

Use the other three items—name, birthdate, and birthplace—to further individualize the person. For example, some names suggest types of people. Someone who is flighty might be called Lilybelle. A sturdy, tough man might be named Jake, and a prim, proper woman Victoria. Consult a book of names for ideas.

The birthplace might be significant. Like names, some regions of the country suggest certain types. The rugged Northwesterner or the laidback Southerner, for example.

2. *BACKGROUND*

A. Parents. What were their names? Occupations? What were their outlooks on life?

B. Character's relationship to her parents. Did she get along with them? Was she rebellious?

C. Other significant people: siblings, aunts and uncles, close friends. What effect did they have on the character's development?

D. What kind of childhood did the character have? Generally happy? Sad? Did anything significant happen that affects her in later life?

E. Education. If she attended college, what was her major?

F. What special interests did she develop along the way?

In this section, develop your character up to the time the story takes place. Create her parents and other significant people as fully as you can. Remember, she is in part a product of her environment. What happened to her as a child will surely affect her as an adult.

3. *THE PRESENT*

A. What is your character doing now? Is she following her profession or special interest?

B. Place of residence.

C. Hobbies and pastimes.

D. Friends and associates.

For this section, build on her background. For example, suppose her parents pushed her into a certain profession. Now, as an adult, she is rebelling by doing something different.

4. *PERSONALITY*

A. Points of view.

B. Attitudes.

C. Traits.

D. Mannerisms.

E. Speech patterns.

Here is where you fine tune your character, where you endow her with aspects that will set her apart and make her an individual, flesh-and-blood person. Again, build on the background you have created. Because of her particular upbringing, she will have specific points of view. She might feel, for example, that everything and everyone in life has a purpose. Or she might regard life as a game. She will have points of view about various contemporary issues. How does she feel toward nuclear armament? Toward surrogate motherhood?

Besides points of view, she will have attitudes. She may take a cynical attitude toward women being given fair treatment in the workplace. She may have a positive attitude toward caring for a sick relative. Points of view and attitudes are closely related, and you may have some overlap in these areas. The objective is to establish how the character feels about what goes on around her.

As I defined in the previous chapter, traits are distinguishing qualities or characteristic patterns of behavior. Your character's traits help determine her personality and, as we have discussed, when opposite the hero's will provide a source of conflict.

Give your character particular mannerisms and speech patterns. Does she gesture when excited? Does he have a habit of running his finger inside his collar when nervous? Does she have a pet phrase that shows up frequently in her speech?

Points of view, attitudes, traits, mannerisms, and speech patterns may be used either in positive or negative ways. The hero and heroine will, of course, have more positive than negative characteristics. Villains will have more negative than positive. Therefore, when creating the Personality part of the biography, indicate whether the facet will be used in a positive or a negative manner. That way, you can avoid developing a hero or heroine who is unsympathetic and a villain who is too likable.

Don't skimp on the Personality section. Often it is these seemingly small aspects of character that make a person really come alive for the reader, that make the difference between one-dimensional and three-dimensional characters. Be sure, too, that what you end up with conforms with what you have created as a background. For example, if someone was spoiled as a child, wouldn't he be at least a little self-centered as an adult?

5. What is the character's problem/goal/need? This is important because it gets the plot under way. The story begins when the character takes action to solve a problem, to reach a goal, or to fulfill a need.

The character's need should be significant and one with which the reader can easily identify. It may be related to her profession. In my *The Love Match*, Diana wants to extend her video matchmaking services across the country. We can understand her desire to be a successful business woman. Or, the need may be related to her background, as in my *Yesterday's Promises*. In this story, Andrea's goal to keep high-rises out of her town is motivated by loyalty to her father. His father was one of the town founders and considered their family keepers of the town's heritage. Familial loyalty is something we can identify with. Even if we do not feel it ourselves, we know others do.

You don't have to start at the beginning of the chart and work through it sequentially. Perhaps you have in your mind a clear picture of the person. You can see her walking and talking, but you have not given her a name or a background. That's fine. Start with what you have and work in whatever direction that takes you. Add to or subtract from the chart to fit your needs.

Don't be paralyzed at this stage if you cannot create all the aspects of a character included on the chart. Your characters will grow as you work with them, as they walk and talk their way across the pages you write. You can fill in needed details as you think of them. For now, do as much as you can.

Keep in mind as the story develops that what you have created beforehand may need to be modified. If you find that some aspect of the characterization does not work—for example, a trait or a mannerism seems inappropriate once it is put into operation—change it! Nothing at this point is carved on stone. Creating a character is a process.

Also, remember that you don't have to include in the story everything you know about the person. Use only what is meaningful and necessary to the plot.

Here are examples of a heroine and a hero developed by the above method.

Meg Saunders, twenty-eight years old, was born in Joplin, Missouri, on April 21. She is five feet, two inches tall. Her long dark hair, though fine and unmanageable, is an eye-catching contrast to her white skin. She has green eyes, a slightly uptilted nose, and full lips.

Meg's parents are Guy and Lorraine. She has a brother, Larry, two years older than she. Guy is a general practitioner. He's easygoing and generally satisfied with his life. He feels he's doing something important and worthwhile, even though he's not fabulously wealthy or famous. Lorraine is high-strung and dissatisfied. She had envisioned herself as the wife of a prominent surgeon and is bitter that her husband never shared her ambition. Lorraine has spent her life raising her children and trying to convince them to make something of themselves.

Larry has reacted by dropping out and drifting around the country. Meg has succumbed to her mother's influence; however, her ambition is tempered by the humanitarian attitude of her father.

Meg attended the University of Missouri, majoring in oceanography. At present, she works in a research lab on one of the Florida Keys. She shares an apartment with another young woman, also a researcher at the lab. With her roommate and other coworkers, she enjoys skin diving and sailing.

Meg would like to be taller and sometimes uses her voice to compensate for her short stature. Although her hair is attractive, she hates its unmanageability. However, she doesn't want to cut it, either. She often wears it on top of her head, to control it as well as to add to her height.

Her point of view on life in general is that everyone should be doing something worthwhile; there's no excuse for laziness or self-indulgence. She's tender and caring, but she also can be impatient. When her impatience becomes extreme, she might shake her finger in the offending person's face. A more innocuous expression of her impatience is running her fingers through her hair (when it isn't atop her head).

She sometimes talks too rapidly or leaves out important information, assuming the other person knows as much as she does. She frequently says, "Don't you see?" when explaining something.

Meg is convinced that a tiny ocean organism holds an important key to understanding the development of all life. She is excited about her discovery. Unfortunately, her supervisors do not share her enthusiasm. They have their own projects to pursue. They will not give her the additional funds she needs to conduct her experiments. She has gone to various agencies with no luck. The only remaining source is a government grant. She must have the grant to continue her work. Continuing her work will fulfill her goals of fame and humanitarianism.

Meg possesses the built-in requirements. She's within the age range, she's mature, and she's attractive in a realistic, flawed way. However, she's still an individual. She has a profession and special interests. Her particular background has given her certain character traits, attitudes, and points of view. She has mannerisms and speech patterns that further set her apart. She has a problem to solve that will start the plot in motion.

Meg's hero is Luke Whitfield, thirty-five, born in Tampa, Florida, on October 5. He is five feet, eleven inches tall, with brown hair and blue eyes. His nose is slightly crooked from being broken during a baseball game when he was a kid. He has the build of an athlete, with broad shoulders and chest tapering to a narrow waist and hips.

His father, now deceased, was Hamlin Whitfield, a U. S. senator. His mother Nelda always hated being in the limelight. Luke attended the University of Florida and Yale Law School. He plans to follow his father's career in politics. He has just won his first election as state senator.

Luke is a person who takes his time before making a decision. He weighs everything carefully. He doesn't have a lot to say, but what he does say is significant. He speaks slowly and decisively. "Give me a minute to think about that" is a favorite phrase. Often, the minute turns into hours or days. He worries about appearing too boyish and sometimes wears glasses with plain glass in them just to appear older and more serious.

Luke's goal is to make a name for himself in state government, then move on to a national office. One of his current duties is to chair the committee in charge of oceanic research grants.

Like Meg, Luke fits the built-in requirements of a romantic main character. His background, points of view, attitudes, traits, mannerisms, and speech patterns make him an individual. Luke heading the research grant committee will be an important source of conflict between him and Meg. Their opposite character traits, her impatience and his patience, provide another source.

TO DO:

1. Get to know your characters in their settings. Write a paragraph or a scene showing each at home. At the office. Shopping in a neighborhood store. Include as much detail as you can.

2. Get to know how your characters talk. Write scenes that focus on dialogue. Practice using the speech patterns you have decided on. Perhaps new or different patterns will emerge as you do this.

3. Get to know your characters' thought processes. Write diary entries. Write letters to friends or acquaintances.

4. Get further inside a character by at times pretending you are that person. Ask yourself, what would my character think about the situation I am now faced with? What would she say? What would she do?

In each practice, include the person's particular points of view, attitudes, traits, mannerisms, and speech patterns. These scenes do not need to be part of the plot sequence; they may describe occurrences outside the story. However, you may find later that you can incorporate some of them into the plot.

CHAPTER 4
Developing the Plot

*P*lot may be defined as what happens in the story. It is the sequence of events that occurs as the characters attempt to solve their problems or reach their goals. But plot is more than a recounting of events; a plot must have shape and form. It must have a beginning, a middle, and an end. At the end, a change must have occurred, either in the characters or in the situation. Sometimes both characters and situation are affected. But, if there is no change, you do not have a story.

THE BEGINNING

The beginning of your story must fulfill certain functions. But exactly what do I mean by "the beginning"? Usually, the beginning means the first chapter, but because story structures vary, let's just say that as soon as possible after opening the story, you must:

1. Introduce to the reader the hero and the heroine (or foreshadow whichever one does not appear).

2. Establish the setting.

3. Tell something about the main characters' problems/goals/needs.

4. Have the lovers-to-be interact and establish the conflict and physical attraction between them.

5. Grab our interest enough so that we will keep reading.

Sound like a tall order? It isn't, really. I've observed, however, that writers unfamiliar with the genre sometimes have difficulty with numbers 3 and 4. I've read beginnings that gave me little or no indication of the characters' goals or problems and little or no indication of the physical attraction and conflict between the two. Remember, the competition for your reader's attention is fierce. You must convince her to read your novel rather than another of the multitude she has to choose from. You must *show* her, with interesting characters and setting, with significant problems and conflicts, with a lively and literate style, that reading your book will be worth her time and money.

THE MIDDLE

In the middle, your characters take actions to solve their problems and reach their goals. Each time they try, they meet with opposition. They keep trying, only to encounter worse obstacles. The situations that arise from these actions-thwarted-by-obstacles are the story's complications.

The tension must rise during this part of the story. That is, each time the heroine attempts to reach her goal, she gets closer. Each time she meets an obstacle, it puts her farther away. Stories that have the same level of drama throughout are boring, and one of the commandments of storytelling is, thou shalt not bore the reader!

Keep in mind that you have two main plots to develop: 1) what happens as the heroine tries to reach her personal goal and 2) what happens in the love relationship. In addition, you may have subplots. The hero attempting to solve his problem or the minor characters trying to reach their goals are examples of other possible story lines.

THE END

Your various story lines will require differently structured endings. Chapter 14 deals with specific ways to resolve plots. In this chapter, we'll discuss briefly the elements that may be included in each ending.

1. The crisis. This is the worst complication of all. Things are as bad as they can get and the situation must be resolved, one way or another. Sometimes the character makes a decision that brings about the resolution. Sometimes the resolution comes from another source. All the story lines should have a crisis, but some will be more developed than others.

In the love relationship, the crisis almost always results in the lovers deciding that things will never work out between them and that they must part forever.

The outcome of the personal goal crisis will be determined by how the goal relates to the love relationship. Sometimes the heroine and hero do not attain their personal goals because along the way they realize that what they thought they wanted they don't want at all, particularly if it conflicts with the love relationship. Other times it works out that they can have whatever else they were after and each other too.

2. The black period. Any of the plots may have a black period, a time when it appears all is lost. For the separated lovers, the black period is full of loneliness and misery.

3. The come-to-realize. Any plot may have a come-to-realize, but the love relationship almost always has one. Sometime during the black period, one—or both—of the lovers comes to realize he cannot live without the other after all. Sometimes this involves an admission of guilt about wrongdoing or wrong thinking.

4. The climax. All plot lines will have a climax in which the situation finally is resolved. In the minor plots, sometimes the crisis and the climax are blended into one scene. In the love plot, the climax usually is a separate scene following the come-to-realize. The character who has the revelation seeks out the other to make amends. The two then reunite for the happy-ever-after ending everyone has been waiting for.

5. The denouement. Denouement is a French term meaning "an untying." If you have resolved all the other plot lines before the lovers reunite, you will not need a denouement. But if you still have story ends to tie up after their climax scene, you will need one. Make the denouement as brief as possible. Remember, your story basically is over once the two are together again.

Let's examine the plot of *Friends—And Then Some*, by Debbie Macomber (Silhouette Romance, 1986). The main characters are Lily Morrissey, a pianist, and Jake Carson, a writer. Lily wants to have material possessions and to marry a rich man. Jake wants to have a simple lifestyle and to be a successful writer. He lives on a sailboat and drives a taxi to support himself. Lily and Jake have met before the story begins, but they are friends, not lovers.

Here is an outline of the main events in the story. Each plus leads the character toward the goal; each minus leads him or her away. The "Love Goal" is defined as Jake and Lily's romance.

Event	Personal Goal	Love Goal
Lily takes a job playing piano in a San Francisco hotel where she has a good chance of meeting a rich man.	+	-
Lily meets oilman Rex.	+	-
But she finds Rex unattractive. Jake tells her he has a "feeling" Rex is not to be trusted and convinces her not to see him. (Complication.)	-	+
Jake submits a story to the *New Yorker*.	+	-

Jake and Lily have romantic encounters with each other. (Complication.)	-	+
Jake decides to find a man for Lily and introduces her to a lawyer friend, Rick.	+	-
Lily doesn't enjoy Rick's wining and dining as much as she thought she would. Something is missing. (Complication.)	-	+
Lily and Jake spend more time together. Their physical involvement intensifies. (Complication.) (Since this is a "sweet" romance, they do not make love.)	-	+
Jake sells a story to the *New Yorker*.	+	-
Rick takes Lily to the opera.	+	-
But Lily finds she would rather be with Jake, celebrating his success. (Complication.)	-	+
Lily and Jake become even more involved when they are together. (Complication.)	-	+
Jake decides to stay away from Lily, to let Rick have her.	+	-
But oilman Rex reappears. When Lily goes out with him, Jake follows them all over town and insists on taking her home. (Complication.)	+	-
	-	+

Lily and Jake spend time together, but neither can express real feelings toward the other. (Crisis.)	+	-
Lily accepts Rick's proposal of marriage.	+	-
Jake decides to move away. (Black period.)	+	-
Lily realizes it's Jake she loves. (Come-to-realize.)	-	+
Lily goes to Jake and tells him she loves him, that she has found out "how meaningless diamonds can be." Jake tells Lily he loves her, too. (Climax.)	-	+

At the end of the story, Jake is on his way to attaining his personal goal as well as his love goal. Lily has made a compromise, in that she realizes her personal goal was not what she wanted after all.

Notice that each occurrence that leads toward the personal goal at the same time leads away from the love goal. Thus, the two story threads run opposite each other. Notice, too, that the events alternate toward and away from the goals. This vacillation is an important means of creating suspense. Just when it appears as though the heroine might reach her personal goal, something prevents it. Just when it looks as though she and the hero will be able to declare their love for each other, something pulls them apart.

TO DO:

1. Begin to plot your story. Write a brief paragraph describing the situation before the story opens. Write another paragraph that tells about the problem, goal, or need that sets the plot in motion.

2. For the personal goal plot, briefly outline the following scenes:

A. The actions she takes to reach her goal and the obstacles she encounters in the process. List as many complications as you can.

B. The crisis. Will the crisis show her about to reach her goal or about to lose it?

C. The black period.

D. The come-to-realize.

E. The climax. Will she reach her goal at the end, or not?

3. For the love relationship, outline these scenes:

A. The initial meeting between the lovers-to-be.

B. Scenes that show conflict between the two and scenes that show their relationship progressing toward love. List as many such scenes as you can.

C. The crisis.

D. The black period.

E. The come-to-realize.

F. The climax.

4. Using the above information, make a chart like the one for *Friends—And Then Some*. Make sure the events alternate between attaining and not attaining the goals. But don't worry if at this point you do not know all the events in the story. Fill in as much as you do know. You can add to the outline and the chart as you write the story.

CHAPTER 5
Developing the Subplot

Think of a subplot as a mini story running concurrently with the main story. Basically it follows the same rules: A character has a problem to solve or a goal to reach. As he attempts to do so, he encounters obstacles. At the end, he either does or does not reach his objective. Good subplots are related to and are woven in with the main plot, yet they should be able to be removed without destroying it.

KINDS OF SUBPLOTS

There are several ways to construct a subplot. If the personal goal of either the hero or the heroine is not a crucial part of the love relationship, it may be considered a subplot. In my *The Love Match*, Diana's goal to establish nationwide a chain of video dating services is not in conflict with any aim of Alex's. Alex is one of her customers, though, and her interaction with him affects her progress toward her objective. When their relationship reaches its black period, Diana is so discouraged she decides to give up her business altogether. At the end of the story, when she and Alex have reunited, he convinces her not to sell her company. Although she has not reached her personal goal at this time, indications are that she will. This subplot is related to the main plot, but it could stand alone or be removed without changing the romance-related plot.

Another kind of subplot involves a main character and a supporting character. In my young adult romance *A Dream For Julie*, the main plot concerns Julie's goal to have a boyfriend. She wants glamorous, erratic Eric rather than steady, reliable Steve. Julie's friend Ann sees through Eric and tries to convince Julie to pursue Steve. This conflict causes a breach in Julie and Ann's relationship. The disagreement gets worse as the story progresses, and while it has no definite crisis or separation period it does have a come-to-realize and a climax. It is a story-within-a-story, related to the main plot yet able to stand alone or to be removed.

Still another subplot may be made up of minor characters. In *The Love Match*, Ben Watson and Emma Riley come separately to Diana for matchmaking. Ben views a videotape of plain Emma and decides

25

she's the one he wants to meet. But when the two get together, Ben finds to his dismay that Emma has attempted to glamorize herself with ludicrous results. With help from Diana, Ben tries to convince Emma to be herself. This mini story is related to the main plot in that Ben and Emma's black moment contributes to Diana's decision to sell her business. But the story could stand alone or it could be removed without affecting the main plot.

FUNCTIONS OF THE SUBPLOT

1. A subplot adds depth and dimension to your story.

2. A subplot adds depth and dimension to the supporting characters. Given problems to solve and goals to reach, they become real instead of cardboard.

3. A subplot can influence the main plot. In *The Love Match*, both subplots contribute to Diana's discouragement about her chosen life's work.

4. A subplot helps you to pace your story. By pacing I mean the alternating of fast-action or tension-filled scenes with those that are more low key. For example, after a dramatic scene in which the hero and heroine vow never again to see each other, place a calmer scene involving a minor character.

5. A subplot can provide a change of tone. For example, in *The Love Match*, Ben Watson and Emma Riley's romance offers comic relief as well as supports the main plot.

Do all romance novels need subplots? Series romances range in length from 50,000 to 85,000 words. Certainly in the longer books you'll need a subplot. In the shorter books, I have found stories both with and without subplots. Sometimes the romance relationship is sufficiently complex to carry the story. Most of the time, however, you'll want to add another story line. I include one or two such mini stories in each romance I write.

CAUTIONS

1. Don't wait too long to introduce the subplot or at least to foreshadow it. I try to include some reference to a subplot in the opening chapter.

2. Don't forget about the subplot as the story goes along. Work it in intermittently. On the other hand, don't let it dominate the story. If it does, perhaps you should rethink your plot.

SAMPLE SUBPLOT

To further understand the nature of subplotting, let's follow Ann and

Julie's subplot in *A Dream For Julie*. This mini story is introduced at the end of the first chapter. The two girls are skiing on the beginners' slope when Eric runs into Julie. He gets to his feet and, after a few words to her, skis off. Julie is thrilled; she has now met the man of her dreams. But Ann has a different attitude:

> *". . . He could've helped you put your ski back on."*
>
> *Julie glanced down. She had completely forgotten about her ski. Still attached to her boot by the leather runaway strap, it lay on its edge in the snow. "He was probably in a hurry to get somewhere. I held him up by causing this dumb accident."*
>
> *"I'm not so sure it was all your fault," Ann said as she bent to help Julie place the ski under her boot. "He was traveling awfully fast. . . . Fast skiers are supposed to slow down when they reach Daisy. . . ." (p. 10)*

The next day Julie and Ann go to the shopping mall. Julie buys a peacock feather to replace the one on Eric's cowboy hat that was ruined when they had their collision. Ann admonishes her:

> *"Julie, I . . . hope you'll be careful. With Eric, I mean . . . that is a fast crowd he runs with."*
>
> *Julie's chin shot up. "What do you mean, fast? Because they go to discos and have after-hours ski parties in their vans? . . . "*
>
> *"I just don't want you to get hurt, that's all." (pp. 26-27)*

Julie is more defensive of Eric than she was in the first scene, which increases the conflict with Ann. In the next chapter, Steve, a boy who is interested in Julie, gives her a book on skiing. Ann says:

> *". . . He seems so nice. And he's obviously interested in you."*
>
> *"Oh, come on, Ann. So he loaned me a book. A friendly gesture, that's all." (pp. 32-33)*

The next time they go skiing, Eric takes Julie, still a beginner, up a steep slope. His friend comes by, and the two boys leave Julie to ski down by herself. The following day Julie and Ann talk on the telephone:

> *"You mean Eric just left you up there on Thunderbird?" Ann was indignant. "Well, I think that's really rude—and dangerous."*
>
> *"You've got it all wrong, Ann. He didn't leave me up there. He had to go to practice. I just couldn't ski well enough to go down with him. . . ." (p. 52)*

The girls hang up, and:

> *Miserable, Julie went back to bed. Everything was going wrong. She and Ann had almost had a fight, something they'd never done before. (p. 52)*

On page 61 Ann chastizes Julie for paying for Eric's lunch. Then Ann secretly invites Steve to be Julie's guest at a special lunch put on by the girls' foods class. Julie is angry at first, but later she cools off and tells Ann, "Let's forget it, okay?" (p. 71). I wanted to show the vacillation in their relationship, how they come together in agreement only to be split apart again by their opposite feelings for Eric.

Julie makes progress with Eric and, although they've never been on an actual date, considers herself his girlfriend. Shortly after their first kiss, Julie telephones Ann:

> *She wanted to tell Ann about kissing Eric, but now didn't seem the right time. Her friend was so distant, somehow. (p. 96)*

Ann and Julie are in charge of a refreshment booth for the ski area's Winter Carnival, which keeps them in each other's company. They get together for an overnight at Ann's house to practice making the pancakes they will sell at the carnival. The conversation turns to the subject of boys:

> *[Ann said] "Are you going to let [Eric] run your life?"*
>
> *"He doesn't run my life, Ann." Julie was taken aback by her friend's emphatic statement. (p. 113)*

The argument escalates and when the two go to bed:

> *Julie lay there stiffly. . . . She didn't want to argue with Ann. Ann was her best friend. What would she do without Ann? (p. 115)*

In the following chapter:

> *. . . Both carefully avoided any mention of boys and concentrated on the Winter Carnival instead. Even so, ghosts of . . . Eric and . . . Steve seemed to hover in the air, making Julie uncomfortable. Ann seemed edgy, too. (p. 121)*

Although the girls still associate with each other, this is the subplot's black period. In the next to last chapter, Julie has her come-to-realize and sees Eric for what he is, self-centered and deceiving. She thinks:

> *"You let him run your life," Ann had said. She decided that Ann had been right. It was a wonder she hadn't given up her skiing entirely to please him. Thank goodness she had not! (p. 128)*

And, finally, in the last chapter, comes the subplot's climax. Julie is with Steve at a party, and Ann and her boyfriend, Tom, arrive:

> *[Julie] had some misgivings about seeing Ann. Would Ann rub it in that she wasn't with Eric? Would she say, "I told you so"? . . . When Ann first saw Julie her face registered surprise, then it relaxed into a welcoming smile. She rushed over and gave Julie a hug. "What a nice surprise! Wow!"*
>
> *"Oh, Ann." Suddenly Julie wanted to cry.*
>
> *"I know." Ann patted her shoulder. "Listen, we'll talk it over later. Just try to have a good time tonight, okay?"*
> *(p. 134)*

Their conflict is resolved, and Julie and Ann are firm friends once again.

TO DO:

1. In the published romances you're reading, focus on the subplots. Which kinds of subplots does the author use? Follow one or more of them throughout the book. Is it worked in at relatively even intervals? What relationship does it have to the main plot? Can it stand alone? What would happen to the main plot if the subplot were removed?

2. To get ideas for subplots, delve into the lives of your minor characters by making a character biography for each of them.

3. Make outlines of all your subplots, similar to the one you made for your main plot.

Notes

CHAPTER 6
Understanding the Romance Style

*S*tyle is an elusive term that often means different things to different people. *The American Heritage Dictionary* (Houghton Mifflin, 1983) defines style as "a customary manner of presenting printed material, including usage, punctuation, spelling, typography, and arrangement." English professor James McCrimmon (Leo Hamalian, *The Shape of Fiction*, 1978, 417) says style is "the pattern of choices the writer makes in developing his or her purpose." Dean R. Koontz (*How to Write Best Selling Fiction*, 1981, 207) calls it "the author's essence, the thing about his prose that makes it uniquely his and nobody else's." Theodore A. Rees Cheney (*Getting the Words Right: How to Revise, Edit and Rewrite*, 1983, 130) states that style is "all the things we do to express our thoughts."

Whether or not you are aware of it, if you have done a fair amount of writing, you already have a style. You tend to use certain words and arrange them in certain ways. For example, some writers use common words and short, simply constructed sentences, while others favor unfamiliar words and complex sentences. Some writers express themselves so uniquely that we easily recognize their works. Ernest Hemingway is one of these highly individualized stylists. So are William Faulkner and John Steinbeck.

Some types of stories have stylistic trademarks, too. Confession stories are told in the first person in a conversational tone. Hardboiled detective stories have terse dialogue and little showing of emotion. "Slick" magazine stories use sophisticated dialogue and vocabulary. Similarly, romance novels have certain distinguishing features.

Can style be learned? William Zinsser (*On Writing Well*, 1980, 20) maintains that "style is organic to the person doing the writing. Trying to add style is like adding a toupee. The person doesn't look like himself." He advises the writer to "be yourself." On the other hand, Lucile Vaughan Payne (*The Lively Art of Writing*, 1965, 69) says that style "is not a mysterious gift reserved for the lucky few. It is something you learn."

31

I believe that both individual and genre styles can be learned. The best way to develop your individual style is to master the rules of good writing. Study word usage, sentence construction, and paragraph development. Learn the techniques of story writing, such as how to develop character, how to write dialogue, and how to build tension and suspense.

To learn how to write a particular genre, analyze it, identify the stylistic requirements, and then consciously practice them when you write. Don't worry about smothering your own style or ruining it for another kind of writing. Your individuality will emerge within the confines of the genre, and because you are conscious of what you are doing, you will be able to modify your style again when you need to.

As you study and practice the following romance style requirements, keep in mind that their purpose is to develop an emotional bond between the reader and the story's heroine. The reader wants to experience the heroine's life as though it were her own. The more you can emotionally involve the reader, the more you will hook her into the story.

CHARACTERISTICS OF THE ROMANCE STYLE

1. Romances are told from a subjective viewpoint.

Stories may be told *objectively* or *subjectively*. An objective narrative has only the facts, like a newspaper article. We do not enter a character's mind to know what he is thinking and feeling. We must deduce the character's feelings from what he says and does. Here is an example of objective writing:

> *Mark's lips came toward Lisa's. In the next moment, he was kissing her. The kiss lasted for several minutes, then he drew away.*

We know what has happened, but we do not know how either character feels about it. Let's look at the kiss again, from Lisa's subjective viewpoint:

> *As Mark's lips touched Lisa's, rivers of fire swept through her. She wanted him, but she knew she couldn't have him. Not now. Her hands came up and pressed defensively against his chest, but his arms, banded around her, held her close. She couldn't fight him, no matter how much she tried.*

Now we know how Lisa feels. We know that although she wants Mark, something keeps them apart. The phrase "rivers of fire" helps to convey the extent of her desire.

Here is the same experience from Mark's subjective viewpoint:

Mark took Lisa in his arms and kissed her. As the hunger inside him grew, he clutched her tighter. She tried to push him away, but he hung on. Why was she fighting him? Hadn't he done what she wanted him to do? What was holding her back?

Now we know how Mark feels, how he wonders about Lisa's resistance. We have experienced the kiss from the viewpoints of both participants.

Some romance lines require the story to be told from only the heroine's viewpoint, and others want both lovers represented. (See Chapter 11 for more information on the subjective viewpoint.)

2. Romances appeal to the senses.

One way to involve the emotions is through the senses. Since the writing is subjective, the reader experiences how things look, sound, touch, taste, and smell to the viewpoint character:

While Janice waited for Derek, she strolled around the garden. The roses were just beginning to bloom. There were rows and rows of them: white, yellow, pink, and red. She stopped here and there to drink in the sweet scent of a bud or a blossom.

But this technique goes beyond simply knowing what the character sees, hears, touches, tastes, or smells. For a deeper bonding, we also need to know how she *feels* about the experience:

While Janice waited for Derek, she strolled around the garden. The roses were just beginning to bloom—like they were at home, she thought with a pang. She bent her head to catch the sweet scent of a red blossom but drew away when she felt tears fill her eyes.

3. Romance language implies sexuality and love.

Words have two meanings. One is the *denotation*, the other is the *connotation*. Denotation refers to what the word actually means, while connotation indicates our associations with that word. For example, "husband" denotes a married man, but it may connote "provider" or "protector." Or, since the connotation often is a highly personal response, the word may suggest to others "responsibility" and "restriction."

Romance writers are careful to choose words that connote sexuality and love. These words may be any part of speech, but most of them will be verbs, adverbs, and adjectives. If you have been taught to go easy on adverbs and adjectives, it may take some conscious effort to incorporate more of them into your writing.

VERBS

In a love scene, the man reaches out to the woman. Your first thought is to write simply, "He touched her cheek." There's nothing wrong with that. It's simple and straightforward. Undoubtedly there will be places in the story where this way of expressing such a gesture is appropriate. However, to get you into the romance style, let's experiment with the verb. Can you think of other verbs that are more sexually charged? Consider these:

He *stroked* her cheek.

His fingers *caressed* her cheek.

He *massaged* her cheek.

A sentence like "He gazed at her" is enhanced by writing:

His gaze *ravished* her.

His gaze *caressed* her.

His gaze *captivated* her.

His gaze *roved over* her.

"She held his hand" becomes:

Their fingers *entwined*.

She *laced* his fingers with her own.

Her hand *grasped* his.

Her hand *enfolded* his.

ADJECTIVES

An adjective describes a noun. It distinguishes the object from others in the same category. If you write "A man entered the room," each reader will conjure up a different picture. Some might see an old man, some a young man. Others might visualize a fat man or a skinny man. You must decide exactly what it is about your man that is important for the reader to see. Then use appropriate adjectives to create that picture:

A *gray-haired* man.

A *ruddy-faced* man.

A *young* man.

In romance writing, particularly regarding the heroine and hero, use adjectives that connote sexuality. For example, "a tall, lean man" sounds more sexy than "a tall, skinny man" or "a tall, thin man." Note the difference when sensuous adjectives are added:

Before: His eyes captured hers.

After: His *smoky gray* eyes captured hers.

Before: He wanted to feel her body against his.

After: He wanted to feel her *sweet, naked* body against his.

Adjectives usually are placed in front of the noun they modify; however, there are other ways you can construct sentences with adjectives.

1. Place two adjectives between the noun and the verb:

Before: Her tall and handsome escort was a stranger to us.

After: Her escort, *tall and handsome*, was a stranger to us.

Before: His frozen and exhausted limbs refused to respond.

After: His limbs, *frozen and exhausted*, refused to respond.

2. Use the adjective with a linking verb. In this kind of statement, a form of the verb "to be" links the subject with the adjective:

His voice was soft and succinct.

Her lips were soft and alluring.

3. Turn an adjective into a noun:

Before: He touched her silky soft skin.

After: He touched *the silky softness* of her skin.

4. Add more adjectives in the form of nouns:

Before: The open neck of his shirt revealed crisp dark hair.

After: The open neck of his shirt revealed *a liberal sprinkling* of crisp dark hair.

Before: His muscular thighs rubbed against her silky limbs.

After: The *taut muscles of* his hair-rough thighs and legs rubbed against *the silken expanse of* her limbs. (Elaine Raco Chase, *Double Occupancy*, Candlelight Ecstasy, 1982, 96)

Caution:

1. Don't add concepts that are already in the noun:

precipitous cliffs

yellow daffodils

brownish dirt

2. Although you will find examples in published romances, I would advise against overloading one noun with too many adjectives:

The playful, short-haired, gray and white spotted dog. . . .

The shiny, delicate, red, teardrop earrings. . . .

ADVERBS

An adverb modifies a verb, an adjective, another adverb, or even a sentence as a whole. An adverb indicates time (now, then, today), place (here, there, inside), manner (quietly, hurriedly, calmly), or degree (very, only).

1. Be wary of modifying verbs with adverbs. If the verb needs an adverb to clarify or sharpen it, perhaps you need a stronger verb. For example, "Ralph jumped suddenly upon the burglar" is improved by writing "Ralph pounced upon the burglar." The verb "pounced" is sharper and more vivid than "jumped suddenly." Similarly, "Judy ate her supper quickly" is better expressed as "Judy gobbled her supper."

2. Make sure the adverb isn't redundant. To say "The radio blared loudly" is repetitive. "Blare" means "to sound or utter loudly"; therefore, the adverb is not needed. Another example is "He clenched his teeth tightly." Clench means "to bring together tightly."

3. Be wary of using an adverb to tell how a character says something. Consider the following dialogue:

> *"You're crazy!" he said angrily.*
>
> *"That's what you think," she replied evenly. "You don't even know me."*
>
> *He said quickly, "I know you well enough to say I think you're out of your mind."*
>
> *"In a pig's eye you do," she retorted sarcastically.*

This is an extreme example, but I have seen similar dialogue in published romances. It is all right occasionally to use adverbs in this way, but there are other methods of indicating how something is said. For example, in the sentence "You're crazy!" the exclamation point gives us a clue. And in the last sentence, the expression itself implies sarcasm. Here's a better way to write the dialogue:

> *"You're crazy!"*
>
> *Sarah lifted her chin and said in a calm voice, "How can you say that? You hardly know me."*
>
> *"I know you well enough to say I think you're out of your mind."*
>
> *"In a pig's eye you do!"*

BASIC SENTENCE CONSTRUCTION

To help you use adverbs and adjectives effectively in your romance writing, let's take a look at how sentences are constructed. All sentences begin with basic statements:

Rain fell.
Mrs. Jones is my mother.
The dog barked at the cat.
Freddy gave his teacher an apple.

You cannot subtract from the basic statement and still have a complete sentence, but you can add to it—in two major ways. You can construct a *strung-along* sentence or a *periodic* sentence.

The strung-along sentence is simply the basic statement with some details added to it:

Basic statement: Rain fell.

Strung-along: Rain fell, splattering the window with silver drops.

The string can be as long or as short as you want to make it:

Rain fell, splattering the window with silver drops, filling the streets with puddles.

In the periodic sentence, additional details are added inside the basic statement:

Basic statement: Mrs. Jones is my mother.

Periodic: Mrs. Jones, the tall woman in the white hat, is my mother.

Basic statement: Freddy gave the teacher an apple.

Periodic: Freddy, who had been absent for two weeks, gave the teacher an apple.

You can combine strung-along and periodic sentences, and you can switch around the parts:

Laura, from the top of her head to the tips of her toes, was an irresistible challenge.

From the top of her head to the tips of her toes, Laura was an irresistible challenge.

Here are some examples of how romance writers have used strung-along and periodic sentences:

> *She walked briskly, making the most of her long slender legs. (Rita Rainville,* Family Affair, *Silhouette Romance, 1987, 8)*

> *His legs, moving like pistons, brought him closer to her.* (Family Affair, *p. 9)*

> *The corners of his mouth pulled down, mirroring his acute disappointment. (Cathy Gillen Thacker,* Rogue's Bargain, *Harlequin American, 1986)*

> *The longing to be possessed, insistent and clamorous, raged through her like fire. (Nora Roberts,* Irish Thoroughbred, *Silhouette, 1981, 126)*

The degree to which you embellish your writing with adverbs and adjectives depends on you. How much are you comfortable with? How many such words can you blend into your own style without having the result look artificial? To give you an idea of the overall effect of embellishment, here are some passages from published romances:

> *Brady stood in front of the fireplace looking down at the*

*blazing logs. He was alone. His jacket had been tossed on the back of the couch, the cuffs of his shirt rolled up to his forearms, and his hands rested on his hips. His silhouette, Sara thought, as her breath tangled in her throat, was a bold statement of masculinity. His attraction was potent, dangerous, and not a bit subtle. (*Family Affair, *p. 41)*

*She was wearing a gorgeous, floaty and filmy lavender cocktail dress. . . . The bodice fit her like a second glove, but the skirt was drawn femininely down over her knees. (*Rogue's Bargain, *p. 75)*

He blinked, his amber eyes momentarily puzzled, and his grip on her shoulders eased. Alida's heart pounded as she stared at his hard-planed face so close to hers, at his generous mouth, sensitive and inviting, a mouth that belied the angry glint in his eyes. (Diana Stuart, The Shadow Between, *Silhouette Desire, 1986)*

[Padgett] grew powerfully, perilously aware of everything he had seen of her: the soft allure of her throat, her wrists, her ankles, her toes in sheer stockings and slender-heeled shoes. (Linda Shaw, December's Wine, *Silhouette Special Edition, 1982)*

TO DO:

1. Make lists of words that connote sexuality and love. Here are some suggested arrangements:

A. Arrange the list according to the various parts of speech, such as nouns, verbs, adverbs, and adjectives.

B. Use a synonym arrangement in which you list all the sensuous synonyms you can think of for words like "touch," "look," "kiss."

C. List nouns used frequently in romance writing, then list adjectives that might be used with them. For example, under "voice" you might include "honey-laden," "husky," "silky," and "tremulous."

2. Practice the romance style on the following sentences. Incorporate as many of the ideas in this chapter as you can: a subjective viewpoint; an appeal to the senses; sensuous verbs, adjectives, and adverbs; and strung-along and periodic sentence constructions.

A. Mike watched Laura walk across the room.

B. Stephanie put on her best dress for her date with Larry.

C. When Tom finally called, Sue thought how good it was to hear his voice again.

D. As they walked along the path, Jason took Alice's hand.

PART II

Writing the Story

CHAPTER 7
The Beginning

$\mathcal{B}$ efore you read this chapter, review the functions of the beginning in Chapter 4. Then, with those in mind, we'll discuss specifically how you will structure your opening.

WHERE TO START

"Where should I begin?" This question will confront you anew each time you sit down to write a story. The answer is crucial. We can't underestimate the importance of the first chapter, of the first page, or even of the first sentence. The sooner you hook your reader into the story, the better.

To determine where to start, regard the narrative you're about to write as a series of events in the life of your main character. She existed before these events began and she will live on afterward. Think of your character's life as being relatively stable before the story begins. Things are going along the way they do for most of us most of the time. Then something happens that upsets that balance. It could be something in her external world, such as a death in the family or a promotion on the job. Or perhaps something in her internal world triggers the situation. She decides to move to a new town or to leave her spouse. Whatever, she now has a problem to solve, a goal to reach, or a need to fulfill. How she attempts to cope with this new situation and the eventual outcome of her endeavors are the story.

Be aware that the event that triggers the plot does not have to be the point at which you begin writing. You have three choices. You may open the story 1) before the important event, 2) during the important event, or 3) after the important event.

BEGINNING BEFORE THE IMPORTANT EVENT

I'll use as an example my mystery novel *Deadly Illusions*. The main character is Jim Meacham, an insurance investigator. In this adventure, Jim probes the death of rock singer Nadine Larrell. Her death, which happens onstage during a performance, is the event that starts the plot in motion. This occurs in Chapter 2.

In Chapter 1 we meet Jim and two supporting characters, coworkers Alex Fletcher and Stella Hooper. Alex gives Jim two tickets to a rock concert that evening. Jim asks Stella to accompany him. The chapter ends with Jim and Stella on their way to the show.

I chose to open the story at this point for two reasons. One, I wanted the reader to get to know Jim before the significant event occurs and thereby to become bonded to him. Placing him in his office environment, in a relatively stable situation, enabled me to reveal something about his lifestyle, goals, and philosophy. However, I did drop hints about the story to come. Both Alex and Stella have knowledge of the rock group, and what they tell Jim foreshadows disaster.

The other reason for opening at this point is that the important event, Nadine's death, has good dramatic value. I wanted the reader to witness this occurrence, and, since the story is told only through Jim's viewpoint, I had to have him present, too.

You don't have to wait until Chapter 2 to show the important event. In fact, don't wait any longer than necessary. Readers want to get on with the story. My contemporary romance *The Love Match* has only a short introduction to the main character. In this story, Diana Winslow owns a video dating service. Alex Skopulos is a new client who causes Diana all sorts of problems, including, of course, those of the heart. Diana managing her business is the relatively stable situation; her meeting Alex is the significant event. The story opens with Diana entering her office on a particular morning. We are introduced to Diana's coworker and several minor characters who form a subplot. Then, on page 3, enter Alex, who starts the plot in motion:

> *In the waiting room, Diana was surprised to find a man; she'd thought the new clients were both women. His back to her, he was studying the pictures on the wall. All she was conscious of initially were his broad shoulders encased in dark-brown suede. Shifting her glance, she saw that the rest of his outfit consisted of snug-fitting Levi's and cowboy boots. Thick black hair grazed the collar of his jacket.*

BEGINNING DURING THE IMPORTANT EVENT

Let's go back to *Deadly Illusions*. If I had chosen the important event as the opening, I would have begun with the rock concert. This would plunge the reader into the middle of the action. Action scenes are good hooks. Mystery as well as romance novels are told primarily through action and dialogue; therefore, this would seem a good choice for a beginning.

There are, however, a couple of disadvantages. One, you're asking the reader to become involved with characters he doesn't yet know, and if you interrupt the scene with too much information about who these people are and why they're doing what they're doing, you risk losing the scene's dramatic impact.

Two, sometimes considerable time elapses between this important event and the next significant occurrence. Suppose, for example, that your heroine being in an automobile accident is the event that begins the plot. It takes her several months to recover, months during which nothing very significant happens. The next occurrence you want to tell about is her meeting the hero. Their meeting is a better place to begin the story.

But the accident has dramatic value, you say, and you don't want to omit it from the story. Perhaps you could use it as a prologue. The prologue form originated with the plays of ancient Greece. At the beginning of the play, a speaker would come onstage and announce facts that the audience needed to know to understand the play itself. Later writers adapted the device to their works. Some of Shakespeare's plays include prologues, and Chaucer used the technique in his *Canterbury Tales*.

A prologue to a romance novel, especially when it leaves the reader wondering what happens next, can be an excellent hook as well as a way of presenting the significant event. But keep it brief. If you find your prologue extending more than a few pages, you may need to rethink your story's structure.

BEGINNING AFTER THE IMPORTANT EVENT

I could have started *Deadly Illusions* after Nadine Larrell's death when Jim is assigned to the case. Then I would have had to let the reader know about the event through a flashback. No problem. I could have accomplished that through dialogue or through Jim's thoughts. As I stated, however, the death was dramatic, and I wanted the reader to witness it.

In my romantic suspense *Home For the Heart* (Manor Books, 1979), Elaine Ellis is away from home when she learns of her aunt's stroke, the event that sets the plot in motion. This occurrence might have dramatic value, but since Elaine as the viewpoint character does not witness it, I chose instead to open after she has returned home and is en route to visit her bedridden aunt.

Not all events that start the plot in motion are dramatic. Sometimes the event is nothing more than the main character making a decision about something, usually a decision to take a particular action. Since decision-making is an internal process, opening with a character talking to himself—unless you're Shakespeare and your character is a Hamlet— makes dull reading. You could have the main character engage in a decision-making conversation with a supporting character, but this, too, is risky.

It is better to open after the decision has been made. I used this structure for my young adult romance *A Dream For Julie* (Berkley, 1985). Prior to the story's opening, Julie has made two decisions: to learn to ski and to get to know Eric Ransom. The two goals are compatible because Eric is a champion skier. The first scene takes place on the ski slopes as Julie and her friend Ann Morton board the chair lift. This is the next significant event that follows her decisions. The scene ends with Julie meeting Eric. Now she is on her way toward reaching both her goals.

THE APPEARANCE OF THE HERO

The appearance of the hero may influence your decision about where to begin your story. In a contemporary series romance, the hero needs to be on scene as soon as possible. If he is the significant event or part of it, then obviously this is where you should begin your story. If the heroine has known the hero before the beginning, perhaps showing something about that relationship in a prologue would work. If he enters the story after the significant event, open with or as close to their meeting as possible and work in the significant event through flashback.

If he cannot be part of the opening scene, foreshadow his appearance. However, avoid this scenario: The heroine is on her way to meet the hero. She thinks about him, thus foreshadowing his appearance and their relationship. All well and good. But she has never met him, and because of what she has heard about him, she envisions him as 1) unattractive, 2) an ogre, 3) a wimp, or 4) a combination of these. Then, unexpectedly, she encounters a devastatingly handsome man. For a while, she does not know his identity. Eventually she finds out that he is—guess who? The hero, of course. This has been done often enough to be cliché. You can be more original.

Still another way to get the hero on scene early in the story is to open in his viewpoint. As we have discussed, it is acceptable to use both hero and heroine to tell the story.

HOW TO BEGIN YOUR STORY

You have decided where to begin writing, but you still don't know exactly *how* to begin. Should you start with characters engaged in dialogue and action? With a character alone? With some details of setting? Let's explore each option.

1. Opening with characters engaged in dialogue and action.

Since romance novels are comprised mainly of action and dialogue, it's not surprising that many of them begin this way. Here's the opening of *A Dream For Julie*:

> *"I hope this is all worth it," Ann Morton remarked as she fastened on her skis.*
>
> *"If you're asking whether we're going to become super skiers, of course we are," replied her friend Julie Atwood.*
>
> *"That, too. But you know what else I'm talking about, Julie," Ann said pointedly.*
>
> *Julie giggled as she pulled on her ski gloves. "Oh, you mean our other reason for being up on this mountain?"*
>
> *"How could you forget?"*
>
> *"Well, looking into my crystal ball, I see you and a tall, handsome man, side by side, doing perfect snowplow turns down Daisy Hill. And me—well, since Eric Ransom's such an expert skier, we'll be up on Thunderbird—provided I do some fast learning."*
>
> *Ann sighed. "The tall, handsome man with me just better be Tom Parkins. But I don't know, Julie; the whole thing sounds like a big order."*

This method insures that your reader learns about the characters by seeing them in action rather than by being told about them. It puts her directly into the main character's life, which facilitates the desired bonding between reader and heroine.

2. Opening with a viewpoint character alone.

This structure will be most effective if you place the character in a setting where she's doing something. Here's how I began *A Love Song For Lani*:

> *Lani Lorimer stood in the middle of Seattle's historic Pioneer Square, searching for a nightclub called Juliette's. Finally she spied it, an attractive, old brick building on the opposite corner. She crossed the street and when she reached the club paused under the neon sign to check her watch. Five minutes to one. She was early. She took a deep breath, hoping to still the butterflies in her stomach. This was an important occasion—an audition for a job as singer with the Adam Young Quartet, one of the most prestigious jazz groups in town.*
>
> *At exactly one o'clock Lani opened the stained-glass door and stepped into the club's foyer. . . .*

Don't allow too much time to elapse before the character interacts with others. In this story, Lani makes her way through the club and on page 2 encounters a man playing a saxophone:

> *When he finished playing and opened his eyes, his gaze landed first on her. But, as if in a trance, he didn't speak.*
>
> *Lani finally broke the silence, saying softly, "I like it. What's it called?"*
>
> *The man seemed to come to his senses. "Sorry, I get really wrapped up in my music sometimes. But the song—I call it 'Adam's Dream.'"*

3. Opening with details of setting.

You may want to take some time at the beginning to set the scene with some details. There are two ways to do this. One is to begin with objective writing to narrate the details, then slip into the main character's viewpoint:

> *On the north side of Lafayette Park, a long stone's throw away from the White House, stood one of the District of Columbia's most imposing dwellings. The handsome mansion was among the showplaces of the nation's capital. Built by the late railroad magnate and financier John Martinson, it was on the sightseeing itinerary of every tourist.*
>
> *Martinson's son, James, had inherited the house and made the most of the stature that being its owner gave him. Standing by the bay window of his study, which gave him a clear view of the executive mansion in the early morning sunshine, Martinson gave vent once more to his envy and impatience. No matter how fine his present dwelling, he reflected, he would not be satisfied until he exchanged it for the White House. . . . (Dana Fuller Ross,* Tennessee, *Bantam, 1986)*

The second way is to work in the details of setting through the viewpoint character's eyes, as I did in *Home For the Heart*:

> *In a car traveling entirely too fast for the uphill curves, Elaine Ellis watched the red and yellow maple leaves glide from the trees and land in the puddles at the side of the road. If she had to come home to Oregon, she was glad it was now, in the fall. She loved the way the deciduous trees blazed here and there like tiny fires on the otherwise evergreen hillsides. She loved the silver mists that hung in the morning air. She wouldn't even mind the predominance of rainy days; the rain, she felt, would comfort her.*
>
> *Tires squealed as the car skidded around a tight curve.*

"Tracy, don't you think you'd better slow down," Elaine admonished her cousin, who was at the wheel of the sleek, red sports car. . . .

The second method might be better for romance novels, for a couple of reasons. One, we know immediately who the heroine is. The sooner the viewpoint character is identified the sooner the reader-heroine bonding can take place. Two, it accomplishes what I referred to in Chapter 6 regarding the subjective viewpoint: Not only do we experience the world through the viewpoint character's senses, but also we know how she *feels* about her experiences.

In the first example, it's true we do know James's feelings, but not as soon as we know Elaine's. Although this is not a crucial issue, it is one you should be aware of. Experiment, then decide what suits your style of writing and your particular story.

THE NARRATIVE HOOK

In its broadest definition, the term narrative hook refers to any opening, because all beginnings are supposed to hook the reader into the story. Sometimes, however, narrative hook means a particularly startling or intriguing first sentence, paragraph, or scene:

"What if Eden Sommers gets herself killed on this little assignment of yours?" (Rebecca York, Talons of the Falcon, *Dell, 1986)*

Catrina had always wondered if your life really did flash before your eyes when death seemed imminent. (Lee Williams, Almost Heaven, *Second Chance at Love, 1986)*

The reporters descended like a swarm of vampire bats, surrounding the tomato-red Audi before Jamie Garland could even get the door open. (Jayne Ann Krentz, True Colors, *Harlequin Temptation, 1986)*

Courtney took one look at Kace McCord and knew that he spelled trouble. (Mary Lynn Baxter, Shared Moments, *Silhouette Desire, 1982)*

A key to writing these kinds of narrative hooks is to omit information that causes the reader to ask questions. In the first example, we are prompted to ask, who is speaking? What is the assignment? In the second, it appears as though Catrina is about to die. Where is she? What is happening? In the third, we wonder why the reporters are after Jamie. And in the fourth, we want to know just what it is about Kace that makes Courtney feel that way.

WHAT INFORMATION TO INCLUDE

If you omit essential details for too long, however, the reader will be confused and frustrated. Eventually you need to provide her with certain information. We novel writers can use the same guidelines journalists use for their news articles, known as the 5 Ws:

WHO

Who refers not only to the name of the character but also to something about him or her. See how quickly we learn vital information about heroine Susan McCormick in the opening of Annette Broadrick's *Bachelor Father* (Silhouette Desire, 1985):

> *The phone rang for a second time before Susan paused from reviewing the contract in front of her and absently reached for the jangling instrument.*
>
> *"Susan McCormick." Her voice was carefully modulated to sound confident and professional, as befitted a competent corporate attorney.*
>
> *"Mom! You'll never guess who was at school today!"*
>
> *A warm smile appeared on her face and she glanced at the walnut-framed photograph on her desk. The smiling face of her exuberant ten-year-old son stared back at her. . . .*

WHAT

What are the characters doing? What can refer to the particular scene:

> *Mary and Tom ate breakfast.*

What also can refer to the overall problem or goal of the main character:

> *Mary and Tom ate breakfast while on a cross-country trip.*

Both Whats are necessary to know, although we may wait a little longer to find out the overall What than to find out the immediate What. Don't make us wait too long, however, or we will wonder where the story is headed.

WHERE

Like What, Where also has two answers. Where tells us the location of the particular scene:

> *Mary and Tom ate breakfast at the El Rancho Cafe.*

But where is the El Rancho Cafe?

> *Mary and Tom ate breakfast at the El Rancho Cafe. When they had arrived in Houston, they'd checked into the Dunes Motel. The cafe was just across the street.*

WHEN

In a contemporary romance, unless it has some special significance, the year is not identified. You will need to include a When, however, to tell the time of year, the month, the day, or the time of day. In Mary and Tom's story, we add:

> *That morning in June, Mary and Tom ate breakfast at the El Rancho Cafe.*

WHY

For novelists, the Why is the most difficult of the 5 Ws. It seems we either tell too much at the beginning or not enough. Too much Why interrupts the current action and prevents the reader from becoming involved with the story. Not enough Why leaves the reader frustrated and wondering about the story's direction. If the reader gets too frustrated, she will not keep reading the book.

Generally, instead of interrupting the beginning scene with a long, involved flashback that, if it gets out of control, could lead back to the character's birth, work in the Why in bits and pieces. That is, tell just enough of the Why to keep us going. It's like dangling a carrot in front of a rabbit's nose. You dangle it, let him take a bite, take it away, then offer it to him again for another bite. Bite by bite, you lead your reader through your story.

In Mary and Tom's story, we know that they are eating in a restaurant on a cross-country trip. But why are they going on such a trip? An expanded opening might read:

> *That morning in June, Mary and Tom ate breakfast at the El Rancho Cafe. When they had arrived in Houston the night before, they'd checked into the Dunes Motel. The cafe was just across the street.*
>
> *Tom took the last bite of his eggs, leaned back in his chair, and heaved a sigh. "Well, Mary, if we don't find your brother here, I think we ought to give up."*
>
> *"But, Tom, you promised you'd go with me as far as L.A."*
>
> *"Face it, Mary. Sam disappeared twenty years ago. He could be dead, for all we know."*

At this point, a beginning writer might be tempted to go into a long, involved flashback about Sam and why he disappeared. But this would interrupt the current narrative. It is better to work in the necessary details as the story goes along.

TO DO:

1. Analyze the openings of published romances to see what techniques the authors have used and how they have used them. Let's go through the process with the first few paragraphs of Donna Carolyn Anders' *North To Destiny* (Bantam, 1985):

Jennifer Carlyle's gaze fastened on the horizon, where the distant cotton fields and pine-covered hills provided a sharp contrast to the July sky faded by the hot afternoon sun. A slight breeze rippled the surface of the Savannah River, which lazed along beneath the bluff where she stood, a solitary figure. She had never felt lonelier in all of her nineteen years. The breeze stirred the Spanish Moss that draped the live oak tree above her, and for a fleeting second, the moss caressed her sunburned face.

Suddenly, her large blue eyes burned with unshed tears as she thought of her father, who had died three months ago from yellow fever. Fighting to control herself, she turned her gaze back to the Carlyle plantation house, which dominated an even higher bluff above a sweeping curve of the river. The magnificent mansion, with its gleaming white marble columns and tall shuttered windows, had once been a showplace in the Old South.

Not caring that her dirty fingers might leave muddy smudges on her face, Jennifer brushed away a tear that had escaped. "Damn the Yankees!" she cried out angrily. Even though it was twenty years after the Civil War, a war that had been over before she'd been born, she hated the North for destroying Georgia. It was small consolation that the Carlyles were among the lucky few who still owned their plantations. Each year saw them taking a bank loan to buy their cotton seeds and pay the wages of disgruntled field hands.

A vicious circle, Jennifer told herself, her anger choked off by the knot of fear that had been growing within her since assuming responsibility for the plantation. She knew that to break even the crops must yield enough to repay the spring planting loan as well as pay the property tax. She wiped her hands on her skirt, adding more soil to the cotton print. But the crops never did yield enough . . . there was never enough money.

We'll stop here and ask these questions:

A. What was the important event that started the plot in motion? Does the story open before, during, or after this event?

We could say it was the Civil War, but that was twenty years before the story opens. A more recent happening is Jennifer's "assuming responsibility for the plantation." Therefore, the story opens after the important event.

B. How does the story begin?

With the viewpoint character alone. Note that details of setting are presented through the character's eyes and that we also know her feelings about what she sees.

C. Did the author use a narrative hook?

Not if we define narrative hook as a startling statement, paragraph, or scene.

D. Who is the character?

Jennifer Carlyle, a nineteen-year-old Southerner, now mistress of a plantation.

E. What is she doing?

Standing on a bluff, looking over her land.

F. Where?

The bluff is above the Savannah River, in the state of Georgia.

G. When?

In the month of July, twenty years after the Civil War.

H. Why?

She's thinking about her financial problems.

As you analyze, be aware of your emotional involvement and what the author has done to achieve that involvement. In this story, the author has chosen a problem that will be easy for us to identify with. Jennifer is threatened with losing her home. The need for shelter is one of our basic needs; therefore, we can readily sympathize with Jennifer's plight.

Also note how far you had to read to find out all this information. Here, we are only a few paragraphs into the story and already we know a great deal.

2. Write your story's opening. Experiment with the variety of ways suggested in this chapter. Don't be discouraged if the opening has to be rewritten several times. However, even if you are not totally satisfied with your efforts, at some point leave the opening and go on with the rest of the book. Writing all of it should give you new insights about how to begin it.

3. As you complete each chapter of your book, summarize it in a few sentences. This will give you a chapter-by-chapter outline that will be useful later when you write the final draft and the synopsis.

CHAPTER 8
The Lovers Meet

The initial meeting between hero and heroine is another crucial part of your story. As with the opening, we cannot underestimate its importance. While every aspect of your story deserves considerable care and thought, your book is a romance; therefore, you must give the relationship between the lovers priority.

If you've opened with the heroine, you've already established that she is an interesting, sympathetic young woman with an intriguing, significant problem to solve or goal to reach. Similarly, if you've opened in the hero's viewpoint, we have become acquainted with him and his problem or goal.

The first encounter between the lovers-to-be hooks the reader into the romance part of the story. When the two interact they are physically attracted to each other, but some conflict prevents them from progressing to intimacy and commitment. This unfulfilled desire creates the sexual tension that is so important to these stories. Think of it as a formula: Physical attraction + conflict = sexual tension.

PHYSICAL ATTRACTION

Establish physical attraction by showing how the characters respond _sensuously_ to each other. What sensations do the sight, touch, sound, and even the smell of the lover-to-be arouse in the other person?

SIGHT

Physical attributes are so important in a romance that often the action is suspended to describe the appearances of the main players. Here's how Georgia sees Simon in *Polished With Love*, by Judith McWilliams (Harlequin Temptation, 1985, 17):

> She noted the deep tan of his skin and the inky blackness of his straight hair. A sharp blade of a nose split a face dominated by high cheekbones, and there were tiny lines around his eyes and mouth as if he laughed a lot. But the focal point of his face was his coal-black eyes. Soulful eyes. Knowledgeable eyes that stared at Georgia as if they knew what she'd been thinking. Knew and approved. They glowed

53

*with dark fire as they focused on her mouth in a visual
caress. . . .*

Add spice to the physical description by having the heroine fantasize
about the hero in another setting, as Georgia does about Simon:

*[Georgia's] breath caught in her throat as . . . her mind
supplied her with an image of [Simon] without the trappings
of civilization. The broad, flat chest would undoubtedly be
covered with the same dark hair as the back of his hands
. . . The palms of her hands itched as she imagined the tingling
sensation of her fingers rubbing over those hands. . . .
(p. 17)*

In Virginia Myers's *Sunlight on Sand*, Janet Wingate fantasizes about
Todd Ballard. Note the emphasis on his power, strength, and virility:

*He looked anything but a scholarly type—more a man of
action. She could picture him skiing, shooting the Colorado
rapids, surfing. There was that aura of pure animal strength.
Even as he lounged and relaxed it was apparent. She could
feel it, like some sort of force field emanating from his
splendid body. (p. 29)*

And in *Treasure of the Heart*, by Pat Louis (Harlequin Superromance,
1982, 28-29), Lee Cameron thinks about Burrton Adburee:

*Now she could see that Burrton's eyes were like black velvet
sponges, absorbing much but revealing little. His strong
square chin balanced his broad forehead and although his
nose was thin and straight, his lips were full and sensuous.
If he had been wearing a bandana headband and a gold hoop
in his earlobe, he could have passed for a pirate, ruthless
and demanding yet with a touch of elegance.*

You can include hints of sexual desire. If it is a sensuous romance,
the reference may be explicit, as in *Polished With Love:*

*[Georgia's] mind had no trouble imagining (his hands)
moving caressingly over a lover's body, alternately soothing
and arousing. (p. 16)*

In a sweet romance, the sexuality is more subtle:

*His smile drove interesting creases on either side of his
mouth below his high cheekbones and his compelling blue
eyes crinkled at the corners. For some inexplicable reason
Kezia's legs wobbled weakly and a strange feeling teased the
pit of her stomach. (Lynsey Stevens,* The Closest Place to
Heaven, *Harlequin Romance, 1983, 9)*

In turn, the hero describes the heroine:

> *[Keira's] elfin face framed by its halo of glowing hair had haunted [Mark] ever since he'd first seen her full-lipped pout and teasingly mocking eyes staring out seductively from the glossy pages of the lingerie section of the store's holiday advertising circular. . . . Every line of that strikingly beautiful face and form, projecting an intriguing devil-may-care aura, had captivated him.* (Blair Cameron, Million Dollar Lover, Candlelight Ecstasy Supreme, 1985, 22)

Like the heroine's description of the hero, his of her emphasizes her sexual appeal. As you learned in the chapter on style, word choice and phrasing are important. Words like "seductively" and phrases like "teasingly mocking eyes" convey Mark's feelings about Keira.

OTHER WAYS TO DESCRIBE THE LOVERS

While we're on the subject of physical descriptions, I will mention that there are other ways to show what the main characters look like. You'll need to use these techniques if the meeting between the lovers is delayed while you deal with other aspects of the plot.

Generally it is a good idea to include some details of physical description as soon as it's appropriate after introducing a character. That way, the reader does not imagine a person as a redhead only to find out ten or so pages later that she is a brunette.

1. The character describes herself. Having the character look in a mirror and think about her appearance is cliché, although I continue to see this device in published romances. A better way is to have something in the situation prompt the character to think about her looks. Stephanie James uses this technique in *A Passionate Business* (Silhouette Romance, 1981, 6). Here, Hilary muses on the kind of woman Logan Saber would be attracted to:

> *Hilary was quite certain she didn't run true to (Logan's) type in a number of . . . ways. Her figure could be described as slender, but she was not blessed with either a model's slimness or the voluptuousness of a starlet. A pair of long-lashed amber eyes were probably the best feature on an otherwise attractive but not beautiful face. The face, with its rather firm little chin, a mouth that smiled readily and the candid straightforward expression in the amber eyes, was not made up to any significant degree. Hilary thought she looked exactly what she was: a hardworking, sober, businesswoman.*

Besides being told what Hilary looks like, we also find out something about her character, that she is hardworking and conservative. When possible, have your physical descriptions include indications of character.

2. Incorporate details of appearance with the action. This method requires an objective rather than a subjective viewpoint; nevertheless, it can be quite effective:

> *The expression on Leigh's face remained serenely pleasant. She smoothed back her simple black chignon with a steady hand, but her tone was firm. . . . Leigh's fingers tightened about the receiver until her knuckles turned white. Her smooth skin tensed over the high aristocratic cheekbones, and she cautioned herself about losing her temper. (Linda Shaw,* December's Wine, Silhouette Special Edition, *1982, 14-15)*

3. A secondary character describes the heroine or hero:

> *But Penny was steadily ignoring Jane's attempts to reassure her. . . . Her gaze was now traveling unhappily over Jane's petite figure, garbed in a black turtleneck sweater and dark jeans. Her small feet were encased in black canvas sneakers. In the black shapeless sweater, she looked nearer fifteen than twenty. (Iris Johansen,* Tempest at Sea, Loveswept, *1983, 3)*

> *[Uncle Padrick] continued to stare at [Adelia] while she searched for her voice, his gaze taking in the deep, rich auburn hair falling in gleaming waves to her shoulders, the large, deep green of thickly lashed eyes, the tip-tilted nose and full mouth which Aunt Lettie had described as impudent, the face now of a startled pixie. (*Irish Thoroughbred, *p. 9)*

Describing the hero and heroine before their initial meeting does not mean you cannot show them again through each other's eyes when they do meet. We saw how Jane's friend Penny describes her in *Tempest at Sea.* Here's what hero Dominic sees when he meets Jane:

> *Dominic's gaze returned to Jane, noting the tousled red hair and wide, frightened golden eyes. His eyes lingered for a moment on the swollen pink lips. . . . "Well, I'll be damned. If I haven't caught myself a baby terrorist." (p. 9)*

And, while Uncle Padrick describes Adelia in *Irish Thoroughbred,* when hero Travis meets her:

> *He spun her around, dislodging her cap, and the glory of her hair escaped its confinement to form a fiery cascade down her back. . . . "You may be pint-sized, but you're packed with*

*dynamite," [Travis] observed, obviously amused. He
wondered as he looked over her softly rounded shape how
he could have mistaken her for a boy. . . . (p. 21)*

TOUCH

Another way to show physical attraction is through touch. Somehow,
often by accident, the lovers-to-be touch each other. One of them,
usually the woman, experiences a strange, unnerving physical
sensation:

> *[As he leaned] forward to unlace the wing-tipped oxford
> propped on the incline of her stool, the young man's well-
> kept hand, his strong fingers sprinkled with a fine smatter-
> ing of silky hairs, met hers. "Here, let me do that," he offered,
> quickly removing his shoe. Recoiling from the brief unex-
> pectedly electric shock of his touch, Keira felt the alarm
> system of her senses clamor. (*Million Dollar Lover, p. 16*)

> *When [Adam's] hand enveloped [Lani's]. . . . His touch sent
> tingles up her arm, through her entire body, down to her
> toes. It took all the willpower she could summon not to allow
> her feelings to reflect on her face. (*A Love Song For Lani, p. 3*)

> *[Bligh's] hand held [Kezia's] chin steady while he rubbed
> gently at two dark smears, one above her eyebrow and one
> along her small slightly upturned nose. He gave her nose
> another rub and her eyes opened widely to meet his at least
> a foot above hers, her heartbeats racing in her chest. "They're
> freckles," she said huskily, her voice tight after the shiver his
> fingers had brought to her body had subsided. (*Closest Place
> to Heaven, p. 10*)

SOUND

Usually it's the man's voice that affects the woman:

> *Adburee's voice grated like sand against slate, hiding the
> sensual quality Lee knew was there. Surely this man was
> aware of the power of his voice to intrigue women. Did he
> turn its sensuality on and off at will? (*Polished With Love,
> p. 26*)

> *To [Keira's] delight [Mark's] deep voice matched the strength
> of his solid good looks. (*Million Dollar Lover, p. 12*)

> *His voice was deep and resonant, and flowed silkily over
> her ears. (*Closest Place to Heaven, p. 9*)

SMELL

The sense of smell is not used as often as the other senses, but it certainly can add to the person's physical appeal:

> *Had this office smelled like sandalwood before [Burrton] entered or had he carried the scent inside on his person?* (Polished With Love, *p. 29*)

> *Leigh froze . . . her eyes fixed on the smooth planes of [Padgett's] nose. The lingering fragrance of soap blended with his aftershave. After all these years it still affected her—the masculine smell of him, the driving force of him.* (December's Wine, *p. 35)*

CONFLICT

When you did your planning in Chapter 2, you decided on the conflicts that will keep the lovers apart. Somewhere in the first scene at least one of these conflicts surfaces, squelching all the wonderful sensations brought about by the physical attraction. Even if you've foreshadowed the conflict in an earlier scene, it still needs to be shown in the lovers' initial encounter. Showing conflict makes it more believable and, as we have seen, is necessary to achieving sexual tension.

In Virginia Myers's *Sunlight on Sand*, we learn in the opening scene that Janet's archaeologist father has died from a stroke while exploring a tomb in Egypt. Janet blames the Ballard Foundation for his untimely death. They refused to refund his project, thus depriving him of his life's work. Therefore, when Janet meets Todd Ballard, she is ready to hate him. But, as we saw above, she is physically attracted to him. Later in the scene, however, the conflict appears:

> *"Dr. Ballard," Janet said . . . "did you have to monitor ongoing funding plans, too?"*

> *There. She had asked it. Now she had identified the cause of the growing dread in her mind. Was this the man . . . who had halted the funding of her father's project? She had to know.*

> *". . . Yes. We—the foundation—always have a number of open-ended grants going, and I learned at an early age that things that are absolutely under control in the morning can manage to fall apart in your hands by noon. . . . I hated like hell to halt the project, but . . . you do what you have to do. . . ."*

> *Janet felt sick. He, this arrogant man in front of her . . .*

*had taken another man's whole life in his careless hands
. . . . (p. 23)*

With this exchange, the conflict we heard about earlier is now more real because it is shown. And it is a significant conflict. Who would not be angry about her father being wronged?

In Nora Robert's *Irish Thoroughbred*, Adelia has come from Ireland to America to join her Uncle Padrick, who works on a Maryland horse training farm. Uncle Padrick takes the liberty of hiring Adelia to help with the horses. Shortly after her arrival, she encounters owner Travis Grant. They meet in the stable, and she tells him she's come looking for Majesty, one of Grant's horses:

> *"Majesty's a very high-strung animal," Travis admonished,
> his gaze roaming over [Adelia] from top to bottom. "You'd
> best keep a respectable distance."*
>
> *"And how will I be doing that?" she demanded imperiously,
> disconcerted by his masculine appraisal. "I'm to be exercising
> him regularly."*
>
> *"The devil you are!" His eyes rose to hers and narrowed.
> "If you think I'd let a slip of a thing like you on my prize
> colt, you've lost your senses." (p. 24)*

Adelia now has to prove to Travis that she is capable of handling his horses, especially his prize colt. Notice how the author skillfully has combined both conflict and physical attraction in this exchange.

In Stephanie James's *A Passionate Business*, Hilary's father wants to sell his restaurant chain with Hilary as a part of the bargain. None of the candidates so far have suited her, and she has no reason to think Logan Saber will be any different. She goes to see Logan to discourage him from going along with her father's game. She finds him unnervingly attractive and sparks fly between them. Nevertheless, she explains her father's plan to Logan, expecting him to go along with her wish to foil it. But his response is not what she hoped:

> *"I'll keep our discussion in mind." Logan paused holding
> her hand a moment longer than necessary. "And having
> promised to do so, may I suggest we celebrate our little
> understanding with lunch? . . ." (p. 17)*

Hilary agrees to have lunch with him, and later, at the restaurant, the chapter ends like this:

> *[Hilary said] ". . . You and I understand each other, I think.
> You will either find another way to buy the restaurants from
> my father or you'll give up the project altogether."*

There was a pause before Logan said in his soft growl, "Yes,
Hilary Forrester, I think I'm beginning to understand you.
But I'm not too sure you understand me." (p. 24)

We know that Hilary still hasn't convinced Logan to go along with
her plan, and because we have seen their attraction to each other,
we know that achieving her goal won't be easy.

TO DO:

Write a scene showing the initial encounter between your hero and
heroine. Incorporate all the senses to enhance the physical attraction.
Show at least one conflict.

CHAPTER 9
Scene by Scene

*Y*ou have written the beginning of your story. You have introduced the characters and identified their goals and any other important issues the story deals with. The hero and heroine have had their first encounter, and sexual tension has been established by showing their attraction as well as their conflict. Now you are ready to write the middle of the story.

In the middle, the characters attempt to solve their problems and reach their goals. As they do so, they are faced with obstacles. The obstacles create new situations, called complications. As each obstacle is overcome, another, more serious one replaces it. The characters approach their goals or solutions only to be thrust away from them toward defeat. In the love relationship, if the hero and heroine are not already in love with each other when the story opens, they fall in love now. They come together, are pulled apart by conflict, come together again, and so forth. For a review of the vacillation that takes place in the middle of the story, see the sample plot chart in Chapter 4.

Writing the middle is difficult. You must continue to delight, entertain, and surprise the reader. You must keep her not just wondering but *having to know* what happens next, so that she will stay with the story. I'm sure we've all become bored with a story that had a promising beginning. We ask ourselves, do we stick with it, hoping it will improve? Or should we put it aside and begin another one? Those of us with persevering natures might go on, but even if we do, chances are we won't choose another book by that author. Don't let that happen to your story!

A story is told in two ways: through narration and through action. Narration is where you, the author, *tell* what happens. Action is where the characters *show* the reader what happens. They appear as though on a stage and act out those particular moments of their lives.

Units of action are called *scenes.* Here is the same event told first through narration and then shown in a scene:

Narration:

When Jim came home that night he was very angry. He

61

> *told Selina he was not going back to that job for anything. This frightened Selina, and she tried to convince him to change his mind.*

Scene:

> *Jim stomped into the room, slamming the door behind him. "I've had it with that job, Selina. Tonight was the last night my boss will push me around. Tomorrow, I'm handing in my resignation."*
>
> *At his words, Selina suddenly felt sick to her stomach. "But you can't, Jim. The rent's due at the end of the week and another doctor bill came today in the mail. You've got to keep working!"*

Sometimes, the two are combined; that is, a scene includes bits of narration, and a narrative passage includes bits of dialogue and action. Even though you'll use both narration and scene to tell your story, since romances are action-oriented, most of your novel will be made up of scenes. (See Chapter 11 for more information about narration.)

Scenes come in different sizes. At one end of the scale are mini scenes, comprised of only a few paragraphs. At the other end are full-blown scenes that may extend for an entire chapter or more. The size of the scene will depend on its importance and its place in the story.

Mini scenes are useful to illustrate a point that you've just narrated or to break up what otherwise would be long narrative passages. Longer, fully developed scenes are like miniature stories in that they have a beginning, a middle, and an end. At the end of a scene a change should have occurred that advances the story. Perhaps the lovers' relationship has altered. Perhaps a decision has been made that leads to the next course of action.

Since romances are mainly about the love relationship between the man and the woman, most of your scenes will show various encounters between these two. Unless they are part of a strong subplot, scenes featuring minor characters should be kept to a minimum.

ELEMENTS OF A SCENE

Time. Let the reader know how much time has elapsed since the last scene: "An hour later. . . ." "The next day. . . ."

Place. This information is especially important if the location has changed from the preceding scene. Depending on the length of the story, include some details of the setting.

Characters. Most scenes have two or more characters interacting. There may be times, however, when you show one character acting alone or experiencing an internal conflict.

Point of View. I think the most effective scenes are told from a single point of view; however, as we have seen, in romance novels it is quite common to jump back and forth from the hero's to the heroine's head within the same scene. The important thing is that the scene have some point of view and not be written objectively. Through the viewpoint character, work in sensuous details: how things look, sound, smell, touch, and taste.

Dialogue. Certainly if the characters are interacting, they will be talking. Most of the time, let us hear their actual words rather than give us a summary of their speech.

Action. Generally the action will be of a physical nature; that is, the characters will be moving around, doing something; but a character thinking about something can be considered internal action.

Not every scene will need all of these elements. The extent of the scene's development depends on its length and its place in the story. However, every scene must have at least one, and preferably more than one, purpose.

PURPOSES OF A SCENE

1. To introduce the characters. Showing characters in scenes is the best way for us to get to know them.

2. To show the character's problem (appropriate if the problem has dramatic value).

3. To show the first encounter between the lovers-to-be.

4. To show how the character attempts to solve his problem or reach his goal.

5. To show the conflicts and obstacles that result from such attempts (the complications).

6. To show the various stages of the love relationship.

7. To show the worst complication of all, the crisis.

8. To show something of the black period, including the come-to-realize.

9. To show the climax.

Let's analyze some scenes, one full-blown and two mini, from my *A Love Song For Lani.* Lani is a singer and Adam is the leader of the group she joins. They have several conflicts. An external conflict is that he favors traditional jazz while she favors more commercial, rock-influenced music. Internal conflicts are her hesitancy to become personally involved with her boss and his hesitancy because of a recent bad marriage. Still another is his disapproval of her extravagance. The following full-blown scene begins after Lani goes to Adam's apartment to deliver soup and sheet music to him while he's recovering from a cold. The chapter ends with a short scene outside his apartment, during which he convinces her to come inside. The next chapter begins:

Adam led Lani through the entryway to a large, skylit room. In the center stood a white grand piano. Around the piano were metal folding chairs, each with a music stand. Leafy ferns hung from the ceiling, and bright prints added a touch of color to the off-white walls.

"Behold the music room," Adam said with a flourish.

"It's charming," Lani said, enviously comparing his elegant piano to her ancient upright. "But don't the neighbors complain?"

Adam unwrapped the new sheet music and placed it on the piano rack. "No. This is an artists' co-op, and most of us are musicians. We have frequent jam sessions. Anybody who's not a musician gets invited to the party. They can hardly complain, then. But come on—let's put this soup away."

In the kitchen Adam placed the soup on the counter. Glancing down at his attire, he said, "Say, excuse me a minute while I change into something more suitable."

"Oh, please don't on my account. I've got to be going in a minute, anyway."

"I know, but I always feel better when I get dressed. Then I know I'm on the road to recovery." Suddenly he sneezed.

She couldn't help laughing. "You sure you're recovering?"

"I'm sure! Be right back."

"Want some soup now?" she said to his retreating back.

"Sure," he called over his shoulder.

While the soup was heating, Lani wandered into the living room, which they had quickly bypassed on the way in. The room looked very masculine with its brown Naugahyde couch and two matching armchairs. In one corner was a sandstone fireplace with photographs lining the mantel. Her pulse quickened. Perhaps this was an opportunity to find out more about Adam's personal life. She hurried to the fireplace and began examining the pictures. One showed Adam and the group outside Juliette's. The others, full of people she didn't know, weren't very revealing.

She was about to turn away when her eye was caught by a half-hidden snapshot. Pulling it out, she saw that it was a picture of Adam, a woman, and a boy of about five or six. The woman, with thick dark hair and classically beautiful features, might have been a model. Although the child had the woman's dark hair, he had Adam's deep-set eyes and full lips.

They were obviously Adam's family. Also obvious, they were not here now. She saw no signs that a woman and child occupied the apartment. What had happened to them? Were Adam and the woman divorced? Did he ever see his child?

Not wanting Adam to catch her being so nosy, Lani replaced the picture and hurried back to the kitchen. She returned just in time to prevent the soup from boiling over. When Adam emerged from the bedroom, she had a hot bowl of it ready for him.

"Mmm, smells delicious," he said, and his happy look made her heart soar.

He now wore navy slacks and a white knit shirt that fit smoothly over his muscular shoulders. She found it difficult not to stare at him as he eased his tall form onto the stool at the snack bar.

He insisted she join him, and she got a bowl for herself and perched on the stool next to his.

Afterward he said, "How about taking a look at the new music? You don't really have to rush off, do you?"

She hesitated, thinking how pleasant it would be to share the music with him. "Okay. But for just a little while."

She played while he sat nearby, offering comments and explanations.

"I had you in mind when I ordered that one," he said when she came to a song titled "Making Believe." "It has a challenging range, and I think you need to stretch your voice."

She sang a few bars of the song.

"Wait a minute," he interrupted. "Let's change that part." He jumped from his chair and came to stand behind her. Every inch of her, from the top of her head to the tips of her sandaled feet, was aware of him. Reaching over her

shoulder for the piano keys, his arm brushed against her. The air between them crackled, and she jumped.

"Sorry," he apologized. "Didn't mean to scare you."

"No, it's not that," she blurted without thinking. "I mean—" She knew he was watching her, but she couldn't look up and meet his eyes. The heat of his gaze, as hot as the summer sun outside, was rapidly melting the wall she had built around herself during the past few weeks.

"Lani."

The ache in his voice nearly stopped her heart from beating. With shaking fingers she played a chord. "Is this the effect you want?" she asked.

"Never mind the song. Look at me." His tone was gentle, yet firm.

"No, Adam, please don't. . . ."

"Look at me, darn it!" He reached out, grabbed her by the chin, and upturned her face.

"So I'm looking. So what?"

"Don't be flip, Lani; it doesn't become you."

In his eyes she saw a sadness so deep and intense that it brought pain to her heart. She had seen such a sadness before in his look. But why?

She wanted to reach out and brush back the lock of hair that had fallen over his forehead. She wanted to trace the outline of his full lips, his nose, his deep-set eyes with their fringe of dark lashes. But she didn't, because she had made a promise to herself not to become personally involved.

Adam bent closer. His lips parted, and a silvery gleam lighted his eyes. She knew he was going to kiss her, and sure enough, in the next instant he reached out to cup her face and pull it toward him.

Quickly she grasped his wrist, stopping his hand in midair. He kept pushing to reach her. He was strong, and she had to summon every ounce of strength to keep him away. Their arms wavered back and forth, then finally he let his drop. "You win," he said with a deep sigh.

It took her a moment to catch her breath. Looking at the floor, she said, "I'd better go."

"Yes, I'm sure you've got other important things to do."

"Uh-huh. I'd planned to do some shopping."

"Shopping? Of course, I should have known. Well, I wouldn't want to keep you away from all the stores."

His voice was so abruptly mocking that she had to look at him to see what he meant by that. "What's wrong with shopping?"

"Oh, nothing." But his tone was cold and distant, and a curtain had fallen over his eyes.

She slid off the bench and stood. To her dismay her knees wobbled. And, worse, he was blocking her way. There was barely a foot of space between them.

"Adam," she said, "I've got to go."

Stubbornly, he stood his ground. She heard his ragged breathing, saw his chest heaving. Why was he staring at her like that? Was he angry, or what? She recalled the snapshot of the dark-haired woman and child. There was someone else in Adam's life. There must be. Yet a moment ago he looked as though he wanted to kiss her. Confused, she ran a trembling hand over her forehead. "Let me by, please."

Still, he made no move. Fighting panic, her glance darted around the room. Seeing an opening on the other side of the piano, she wheeled and fled. She hurried through the apartment, his footsteps echoing behind her. Reaching the front door, she grabbed the knob and turned it, but it was locked, and she waited, breathless, until she saw his hand reach out and unsnap the button.

"When do you think you'll be back?" she managed to ask as she went through the door.

"This Tuesday, for sure."

"Good. We're all looking forward to your return."

In a daze Lani made her way out of the building. . . .
(pp. 60-65)

Now let's analyze the scene, checking it against the list of elements:

Time? We learned earlier it is "the next morning."

Place? Adam's apartment. Notice the details of setting.

Characters? Adam and Lani.

Point of View? Lani's. Notice the incorporation of the senses. The air crackles when they touch. She feels the heat of his gaze. The sadness in Adam's eyes brings pain to her heart.

Dialogue? Yes, between Lani and Adam.

Action? Yes, moving about the apartment. The most important action is between the two, when they touch and when she evades his embrace.

Purpose? Like most full-blown scenes, this one has several purposes. One is to show them getting along, if only for a brief period. Another is to advance the story by introducing the woman and child. This presents a new (to Lani) complication in the development of their relationship. The scene also reinforces two conflicts: her resolve not to become involved with her boss and his disapproval of her extravagance.

The scene has a beginning, a middle, and an end. The beginning presents a relatively stable, almost happy picture of the two. He's pleased that she's come to visit him while he's ill. She's brought him soup and is going to fix it for him. However, an unsettling element is introduced when she sees the picture of him and what she believes to be his family.

In the middle of the scene, they share the soup and then the music. The situation still is pleasant. But the mood changes when he tries to make love to her. She thinks about the picture she saw. She remembers her resolve not to become involved with her boss. These thoughts cause conflict. The mention of shopping reminds Adam that he disapproves of her extravagance. More conflict. Now the two are at loggerheads. But they still are attracted to each other and, as we have discussed, physical attraction + conflict = sexual tension.

Since the conflicts cannot be resolved at this point (if they were, the story would be over), Lani chooses to escape. Her leaving brings about the conclusion of the scene.

Notice that the dramatic level does not stay the same during this full-blown scene. It begins on a relatively peaceful note and becomes increasingly tense after the appearance of conflict.

Most of your scenes will contain conflict, for conflict is a necessary ingredient not only of a romance novel but also of any story. However, there will be times when you want to show the man and woman agreeing more than conflicting. How else will we believe they have fallen in love with each other?

One way to do this is to show them in a peaceful, happy scene, but with conflict an underlying presence, as in this mini scene from Lani's story. Lani, Adam, and the group have gone on tour to promote their new record. One evening after a performance, Adam takes Lani out to dinner, and:

Later, in the taxi heading back to the motel, they both fell silent again, but this time instead of racking her brain for something to say, Lani relaxed. There was no reason why they should keep talking all the time. Then she realized why complete silence with Adam was not a good idea—it made her more aware of the effect his nearness had on her. Her heart was beating more rapidly than usual, and her head had a giddiness that she couldn't blame on the wine.

The cab turned a sharp corner, and she fell against Adam, her shawl sliding from one shoulder. As he replaced the wrap, he drew her to him.

She caught her breath. "Adam—"

"Shh," he whispered against her ear while slipping his other arm around her waist. "Don't say anything. I just want to hold you."

Lani wasn't content with being held. She longed to have his lips crush hers with fiery kisses; she ached for the touch of his sensitive fingers. But she reminded herself that this was better than nothing. At least they weren't fighting. So she forced herself to lean quietly against him, encircled by his arm.

"Driver," Adam said, "take us back the long way." (pp. 106-7)

Here, the conflict is within Lani. Adam is holding her but she isn't content. "She longed to have his lips crush hers with fiery kisses. . . ." The purpose of this mini scene is to show a new stage in Lani and Adam's relationship. She does not refuse his touch, as she does in the earlier scene, but allows him to put his arm around her. Yet, even in this agreeable situation, conflict is present.

Here's another, later mini scene without conflict:

"Do you think Leo really will?" Lani asked Adam that night as they stood in front of her hotel door.

"Leo who?" Adam buried his face in the soft curve of her neck.

"Leo-the-disc-jockey," she replied patiently.

"Oh, him. Will what?" Adam's lips trailed kisses up her neck and across her cheek.

"Will send his friend our record."

"Mmm, delicious. I don't know. Maybe if he can stop talking long enough to put it in the mail."

Lani giggled. "I thought he was nice."

"He was a babbling jerk. And you're talking too much, too. But I know a way to stop that."

"Oh, Adam . . ." she managed to whisper before his kiss swept her away. (p. 116)

In this scene, the lovers are close to resolving their differences. It's not time for the story to end, however, and in the next scene conflict drives them even farther apart. Keep such no-conflict scenes brief and alternate them with scenes where conflict is present.

TO DO:

1. If you haven't already done so, list as many of your story's events as you know at this point. Using the list of scene purposes given in this chapter, decide which events to narrate and which to show in scenes.

2. After you write a scene, analyze it the way we analyzed the scenes from *A Love Song For Lani*. Notice I said *after* you write a scene. Don't try to keep all these things in mind if you're unaccustomed to composing with this kind of awareness. I don't want you to get writer's block trying to work in everything when you're initially creating the story. Let a scene come as it wants to come. You can always add to it or subtract from it later.

Also, remember that you don't have to write the scenes in sequence. Write the parts that come to you the most strongly and persistently. You can rearrange and bridge them together later.

CHAPTER 10
Dialogue

$\mathcal{S}$ince most of your romance novel is made up of scenes, dialogue is an important ingredient of your story. To write effective dialogue, you need to know what functions dialogue performs as well as the techniques for writing it.

FUNCTIONS OF DIALOGUE

1. One of the most important functions of dialogue is to show character. For me, characters don't really come alive until they're onstage and I can hear them speak. There are two ways dialogue helps to show character:

A. Through what the person says:

> *"Look, Mark." Jane held out a brown wallet. "I found this in the grocery store."*
>
> *"Take the money out and put it back where you found it," Mark said. "Anybody who can't hang on to his wallet deserves to lose his money."*
>
> *"No way! I'm turning this in. If it were mine, I'd sure want the person who found it to do the same."*

From this exchange we learn that Mark has a "finders keepers" attitude and Jane honors the "do unto others" command.

B. Through how the person says it. Here's an example from *Unnatural Causes*, a mystery by P. D. James (Warner, 1982), in which Inspector Adam Dalgliesh asks a suspect about his whereabouts during a crime:

> *. . . Bryce, wearing a heavy oilskin which reached to his ankles topped with an immense sou-wester, stood dripping and glistening in the middle of the room, like an animated advertisement for sardines. He was clutching a coil of heavy rope with every appearance of knowing what to do with it and had the air of a man dedicated to action.*
>
> *He said:*
>
> *"If there's any swimming to be done, my dear Adam, one must leave it to you. One has one's asthma, alas." He gave*

Dalgliesh a sly elliptical glance and added deprecatingly, "Also, one cannot swim."

Bryce's referring to himself as "one" and to Dalgliesh as "my dear Adam" show him to be a pretentious person.

2. Dialogue can further the action of the story:

"I've made up my mind," Amanda said. "This house goes on the market today. I'm going to call that real estate agent right now."

"Wait a minute, honey," Joe said. "I thought we were going to think about selling for a couple of weeks, then decide."

Amanda shook her head. "We've tried that before. It just means an indefinite postponement, and you know it."

"I wish you wouldn't, Amanda. . . ."

Sometimes dialogue can be used in place of telling what the action is, as in J. D. Salinger's story "Uncle Wiggily in Connecticut" (*Nine Stories*, Little Brown, 1953, 35). Mary Jane is visiting her former college roommate, Eloise. The two are drinking highballs in the living room when Mary Jane says:

"Oh, God! Look what I did. I'm terribly sorry, El."

"Leave it. Leave it," said Eloise. "I hate this damn rug anyway. I'll get you another."

"No, look, I have more than half left!" Mary Jane held up her glass.

"Sure?" said Eloise.

3. Dialogue can convey needed information:

"I was born here," he said. "Just five months after my family moved up from California."

4. Dialogue can show the emotional state of the speaker:

"I've had just about enough," Mike said. "First Jason walks through a glass door and has to have fifteen stitches in his hand. Now he falls off his bike and gets a concussion. Is he accident-prone, or what?"

"Now, Mike," Susan replied, "normal boys are always banging themselves up."

"Yeah. But not like this! I'm beginning to wonder. Maybe there's something wrong with our kid."

5. Dialogue can show conflict:

"Are you telling me we have to go tomorrow night?" Arlene asked.

"That's right," Martin replied.

"I wouldn't be caught dead at that party!"

"You'll go if I say so!"

"Make me!"

6. Dialogue can build reader suspense:

"We'll drill right through the tunnel."

"Yeah? I remember the boss telling about the time he tried that. He was the only survivor."

"The boss hasn't been on the job as long as I have. And I say we can drill through the tunnel."

7. Dialogue can foreshadow:

"I hear he's back," George said.

"Who's back?" Lenore asked.

"Why, Brandon, of course."

"I'm not afraid of Brandon. Is that all you called to tell me, George?"

8. Dialogue can characterize someone through the speaker's viewpoint:

"Did you meet Sarah yet?" Martin asked.

"Did I meet her! She bent my ear for nearly an hour with stories about her ailments."

9. There is yet another function of dialogue that is particularly applicable to romance novels. As we have discussed, to make the developing love relationship believable, you need scenes that show the lovers getting along with each other. One way is to show them engaged in banter. Such good-humored teasing also adds humor to your story, and humor is always an asset.

Here's some banter between Andrea and Jason in *Yesterday's Promises.* The two have just finished a picnic lunch:

"I think I could take a nap very easily right now," Andrea said as they cleaned up the remains of their feast.

"Not on my time." Jason gave her a stern look. "You may lie down, but no napping!" He drew her down onto the blanket and into his arms.

"Mmmm," she murmured. "This is even better than roasted chicken."

"Well! That's the first time I've ever been compared to a chicken. But I'm glad I came off favorably." (p. 120)

Dialogue can perform more than one function at a time; in fact, the more you can make it do, the better. Let's look at another conversation from *Yesterday's Promises*, between Andrea and her brother, Edward. This scene is from the second chapter and marks Edward's first appearance in the story. In the opening chapter, we learn through Andrea's thoughts that she and her brother do not get along well. Now it is the following day and he has come down to breakfast:

> *"I need to talk to you," (Edward) finally said, avoiding her eyes.*
>
> *Andrea's stomach tensed. "Go ahead."*
>
> *"I need some money."*
>
> *"You get an allowance from the trust fund every month," she reminded him.*
>
> *"It's not enough."*
>
> *"How could it not be enough? You don't have any room and board to pay."*
>
> *"Why should I pay room and board here? Half of this house belongs to me."*
>
> *Andrea sighed. "All right, but you know the provisions that Dad set up for the trust fund."*
>
> *"Yeah, but you could make that goat of a lawyer bend a little. He'll listen to you."*
>
> *"Edward, what do you need money for? You've got your big expensive car, which, by the way, you should learn to drive safely. You nearly ran into me last night."*
>
> *"That was your fault. You were over the centerline."*
>
> *"I was not!" Andrea checked herself. There she was, arguing with him again, lowering herself to his level. "Anyway, what do you need money for? You're not in any trouble, are you?" She studied him carefully, but his knitted brows and pouting lips indicated only stubbornness.*
>
> *"I want to make some investments."*
>
> *"What kind of investments? You don't know anything about investing money."*
>
> *"Who says I don't? And it's none of your business what kind of investments."*
>
> *"If you expect me to convince Mr. Dreyfus to bend the rules, I'll have know what it's for."*
>
> *"Oh, all right. Stocks and bonds."*

He was avoiding her eyes again, and she had the feeling he was lying. But if she accused him, he would only deny it.

"The money that's in trust is already invested," she reminded him. "And you'll receive another lump sum when you're twenty-five."

"That's three years from now."

"Instead of spending your time playing tennis and drawing pictures, you could go to work and earn some money."

"Where would you suggest? Down at your musty, boring museum? Not on your life."

"Dad always hoped it'd be a family operation."

"You don't have to remind me what Dad always hoped. I'm sick of hearing it. I'm telling you I want some money. Now. Or else!"

"Or else what? Edward, you wouldn't do anything foolish— or would you?"

"Anything to tarnish the family name? One of the oldest families in old, old Bayport? Is that what you're worried about? What a terrific idea!"

This dialogue *characterizes* Edward by showing his abrupt manner and his calling the lawyer "that goat"; it *shows conflict* between Andrea and Edward; it *conveys information* about the trust fund; it *foreshadows* by suggesting Edward is going to do something wrong with the money; and it *furthers the action* in that Edward asks Andrea for money.

TECHNIQUES FOR WRITING DIALOGUE

1. Dialogue is the *essence of real speech*. That is, not everything people would say in an actual situation needs to be incorporated into the story. In reality, people hem and haw, repeat themselves, and use more words than are necessary to convey their messages. When you write dialogue you must condense and distill what people would really say. Consider the following examples. The first records the actual speech; the second condenses it:

"Hi, Merry," Jack said. "We're having a party tomorrow night—the wife and I. My folks are in town, you know, and well, since they're only going to be here a few days and all, we—the wife and I—figured we'd better get on the ball and have a few people over. If you're not doing anything, we'd sure like to have you join us. It's tomorrow—Friday, that is, and we'd sure like to have you join us."

> *"Hi, Merry," Jack said. "We're having a party tomorrow night—the wife and I. My folks are in town and the wife and I figured we'd better have a few people over. We'd sure like to have you join us. It's tomorrow—Friday. Don't forget!"*

By retaining the casual sentence structure and the repetition of the phrase "the wife and I," we get the impression of this person's rambling speaking style without the wordiness of his actual speech.

2. Even though dialogue is the essence of real speech, it still must sound natural and convincing. One way to make a character sound like a real person is to be selective about his vocabulary. Use only the words that someone of his age, occupation, sex, educational background, and temperament would use *in talking*. We all have three vocabularies: one for speaking, one for writing, and another for reading. Words that we recognize when we read may not be part of our speaking vocabulary. Similarly, words that we use in our writing we may not include in our speech.

In the above example, Jack's referring to his parents as "folks" and to his wife as "the wife" indicate that he is a person with colloquial speech patterns.

Another way to make speech sound natural is to forget sentence structure and rules of grammar. People do not always speak in complete sentences nor do they use proper grammar. Here's a dialogue from Judith Guest's *Ordinary People* (Ballantine, 1982), between Cal and his son Conrad:

> *[Conrad] is conscious now, shading his eyes with his hand against the light. "Time's it?"*
>
> *"Twelve."*
>
> *"You just get home?"*
>
> *"Yeah. What're you doing down here?"*
>
> *"I couldn't sleep."*
>
> *Cal laughs. "I see that."*
>
> *"Time's it?"*
>
> *He turns away to hang up his coat. "I just told you. Twelve o'clock. Let's go to bed, okay? I'm bushed."*

Conrad does not ask formally, "What time is it?"; rather, he condenses it to "Time's it?"

Still another way to achieve natural-sounding speech is to give the characters speech tags. A speech tag is a word or phrase that the person uses frequently, such as Jack's choice of "folks" and "the wife" in the above example. Here's another example:

"You're coming home with me," Monica insisted. "Believe me, when you're down in the dumps the best thing to do is to be with somebody. I should know, I've been there often enough and gone home to my mother."

"Believe me" is Monica's favorite phrase. It will show up periodically in her speech, not often enough to irritate the reader, but often enough to help characterize Monica.

3. Weave dialogue in with the action.

Sometimes the dialogue is an integral part of the action; both are equally important and both are needed to understand the scene. In this scene from *Yesterday's Promises*, notice how both Ned's actions and his speech show his annoyance with Andrea.

It was midafternoon when [Andrea] entered the Bayport Pharmacy. Ned was just finishing with a customer. . . . "Oh, hi, Andrea," Ned said when he saw her. The greeting sounded friendly enough, but she thought it lacked his special warmth. Instead of giving her a quick peck on the cheek, as he often did when the store was empty, he busily began putting some bottles on the shelf.

"Here's your petition." She held out the paper.

"You can just set it on the counter."

She waited while Ned finished with the bottles, but then he started folding some boxes. "Well, aren't we going out?" she asked.

"You're too late for lunch and too early for dinner," Ned said petulantly.

"But just in time for a coffee break. Come on, I want to hear your idea."

"All right. If you're sure you can spare the time." (p. 41)

Other times it's the dialogue alone that moves the story ahead. Still, especially in category books such as romances, it's a good idea to include some action. How often do we talk without doing something physical, even something as simple as pointing a finger or waving an arm? When possible, depict action that supports what's going on in the dialogue:

Marie handed Liz a cup of coffee. "I don't know what I'll do now that Mark's gone. He was the best salesman we had."

"I know how much you thought of him." Liz carefully measured out a teaspoon of sugar and dumped it in her coffee. She stirred it for a moment, then looked up at Marie.

"I don't know how to tell you this, Marie, but when I checked the safe this morning, several thousand dollars was missing."

Liz's careful attention to her coffee lets us know she is having trouble breaking the bad news to Marie. It also slows the pace, a signal that something important is about to be said.

Sometimes writers effectively incorporate the action at the beginning of the dialogue but forget to do so as the conversation progresses:

"I didn't think you'd come back," Jake said, helping Tamara into the car.

Tamara fastened her seat belt. "I wasn't going to, but I had nothing else to do. Besides, I haven't seen Evelyn for a long time."

"I was hoping I was the reason you came."

"Don't kid yourself, Jake. You were not the reason."

"I should have left, too, and gone back to Tucson."

"Huh! It's no secret why you're sticking around."

"If you're so smart, why am I sticking around?"

"Money, of course. You're just as greedy as the rest of your family. . . ."

Along about this time we begin to wonder what the characters are doing. Is Jake in the car? Have they begun their trip? Nothing is moving except their mouths, resulting in a "talking heads" effect.

In scenes where the dialogue is the most important element, you can avoid the "talking heads" effect by adding action that has a beginning, a middle, and an end. If possible, choose an action that is germane to the story. I used this technique in *A Dream for Julie.* The girls' foods class is planning a Chinese lunch. Ann and Julie have decided to practice cooking a coconut custard that is part of the menu. They go to Ann's house:

The girls quickly set to work. Ann sifted the dry ingredients while Julie beat the egg whites into a stiff froth. Their phone conversation on Sunday had ended on a strained note, but now, as they worked side by side, discussing the task at hand, Julie felt close to Ann again. She welcomed the return of this feeling; Ann was, after all, her best friend.

She was bursting to tell Ann about her lunch with Eric. What were best friends for if not to confide in? Still, she hesitated, because it seemed that whenever Eric was the topic of conversation she and Ann drew apart.

While she was still debating whether or not to share her news, Ann said, "Say, I saw you getting in Eric's van today when Tom and I were on our way to the debates."

Here was the opening she needed. "Eric took me to lunch," Julie said, her voice full of pride.

"Well, that was nice of him." Ann poured the mixture into the shallow pan. "There now, into the oven with this mess. So where'd you go?"

Julie launched into an account of lunch at Taylor's. When she got to the part about Eric having only a dollar, Ann interrupted.

"Wait a minute. You mean he asked you to lunch and you ended up paying?" Her green eyes flashed indignantly.

"Well, no, not really. It was just a loan. I'm sure he'll pay me back." Julie fought to keep the defensiveness out of her voice.

"Did he say so?"

"I . . . don't remember."

Ann looked as though she wanted to say more, but she bit her lip instead. "Well, go on."

Julie continued her story, but without her former enthusiasm. Ann's disapproval of nearly everything Eric did was chipping a crack in their otherwise solid friendship. Julie had a horrible feeling that the crack could become a chasm if she didn't watch out.

When Julie had finished her story Ann said, "Are you going to invite Eric to the lunch? We can bring guests, you know."

"I know. But no, I think he . . . has a noontime practice that day."

Ann stared absently at the kitchen timer as it ticked away the minutes of baking time. Then she said, "Steve Neilsen was one of the debaters today."

"Oh, really?" Julie replied, only mildly interested. . . .

"He's really good at it, too," continued Ann. "He's on the same team that Tom is on. The issue they're debating this year is the quality of education. . . . I thought you were interested in debate. Didn't you tell me you were on the team back home?"

"Yes, I was."

"You should really come and watch sometime. It's fun."

Julie shook her head. "It's no fun for me to sit on the sidelines. I want to be in on the action." Then she added, "Oh, I can understand how it is for you—being involved with Tom and all."

"Yeah. I just wish—"

"What?" Julie was struck by the wistful note in her friend's voice.

"Oh, nothing."

Just then the timer went off. Relieved to have this conversation brought to an end, Julie jumped up and ran to the oven.

"Looks fantastic!" she cried, removing the pan of steaming coconut custard. "Smells even better!"

They decided the custard was a success, although Ann ate such a small piece Julie didn't know how she could tell.

In the above scene, it's the dialogue that moves the story ahead by increasing the conflict between Julie and Ann over Julie's pursuit of Eric. The action, which is related to the plot, provides a frame to hang the dialogue on. Think about TV shows and movies. Aren't the characters usually engaged in some kind of physical action while they talk?

4. Weave dialogue in with the viewpoint character's internal reaction to what is said. Letting the reader know what the character is thinking helps to maintain the reader-heroine bond.

"Your son will recover from the accident, Sara," Dr. Graham said.

"I know he will," Sara agreed. He's lying, she thought to herself. I know he's lying.

However, too many internal reactions can interrupt the dialogue, sometimes to the extent that by the time we hear the second speaker's response we've forgotten what the first person said:

Jake gave Tamara a long look. "I was afraid I'd never see you again."

"I was afraid I would see you again," she shot back, turning her face to the window. As the train increased its speed, the trees and bushes blurred before her eyes. "So how did you find me?" she couldn't help asking.

"Your brother. 'Course I had to do a little arm twisting."

Her brother! She should have known. How many times in the past had she been betrayed by Mike? She could remember when they were kids, how he would listen in on her conversations with her girl friends, about the boys they had crushes on. Mike would threaten to tell the boys what the girls had said, unless he was paid not to. When she tried to get their parents to intervene, all they would say was, "You and Mike have to work out your own problems." It had gotten worse as they grew older. She tried reasoning with him. She tried appealing to his better self until she realized he didn't have a better self. Nothing worked. It was enough to make her wish she were an only child.

She said to Jake, "That rat! Well, I hope he got you for plenty."

"It was worth it."

She hated Jake's smugness. He had been smug from the beginning. . . .

You can see how so many thoughts interrupt the flow of the dialogue and therefore disrupt the scene. To avoid such interruptions, keep the viewpoint asides brief and, above all, purposeful. See Chapter 11 for the purposes of narrative interjections.

5. The "said" dilemma. Writers often ask, "Can I write an entire story using the speaker's name and the word 'said'?" Yes, you may. There are many published stories in which the speaker is identified with a "he said," instead of such substitutes as "he mumbled," "he muttered," or "he taunted." However, you may want to use some of these substitutes for variety or to show how the words are spoken. But be careful not to overuse these replacements. If someone is always grumbling or mumbling or snorting, it calls our attention away from the speech itself.

Be aware, too, of the correct punctuation with some of these substitutes. Don't write "Oh, no, you can't," Mary laughed. People cannot laugh and speak at the same time, and these two actions shouldn't be part of the same sentence. Change the comma to a period: "Oh, no, you can't." Mary laughed.

Another technique to show how something is said is to help the verb with an adverb: "Why don't you ever listen to me?" he asked angrily. "You're a jerk," she said sharply. Adverbs are all right, *if used sparingly.* Overuse of adverbs to show how something is said indicates lazy writing.

Perhaps a said substitute would be more precise: "Why don't you ever listen to me?" he complained. "You're a jerk," she barked. Or punctuation might do the job. In "You never listen to me!" and "You're a jerk!", the exclamation points tell us these are sharp, abrupt statements.

There will be times when you will want to use *bare dialogue*, speech without any "said" or said substitutes or adverbs. Bare dialogue is effective especially for showing conflict:

> *"I think you should see a doctor," Mark said, his voice rising.*
>
> *"You know I don't like doctors fussing over me," Mary replied.*
>
> *"But your arm is swelling, for God's sake! It might be broken."*
>
> *"Don't be ridiculous. It's not broken."*
>
> *"You're the most stubborn woman I've ever known. So be a cripple!"*

Notice that the dialogue begins with identifying the speakers and then drops all bits of action and identification for the rest of the exchange. Obviously the speech couldn't go on too long this way or we'd lose track of who is speaking. Use bare dialogue for only the most intense part of the conversation or throughout an entire scene as needed to show the rise and fall of emotion.

To eliminate some of the "saids" or said substitutes, use bits of action to show who is speaking:

> *Tamara slid onto the seat next to the window. A few minutes later, Jake sat down beside her. "Oh, no! How did you find me?"*
>
> *Jake's eyes danced mischievously. "It was easy. I twisted your brother's arm."*
>
> *"I should have known. He's always betraying me." She turned her face away and looked out the window. The train had gained speed and the scenery blurred before her eyes. "Well, I hope you had to pay him plenty."*
>
> *Shifting in his seat, Jake leaned so that his nose almost touched her cheek. "It was worth every penny."*

TO DO:

1. Write dialogues for the following situations. Make each exchange perform as many of the functions listed in this chapter as you can.

A. A married couple discusses the possibility of divorce.

B. A mother talks to her teenage son about his truancy (or some other problem).

C. Two women discuss their feelings for the same man.

D. A couple tries to decide where to go for a vacation.

E. A street preacher attempts to proselytize a passerby.

F. A policeman gives a motorist a ticket for speeding.

2. Analyze each dialogue exchange you have written so far in your story. Which functions does it perform? Can you make it do more?

3. To better understand dialogue and its functions, study plays. Then write your dialogue as if you were writing a play. Remember, in a drama there are few directions that tell how something is said. The words themselves must do most of the work.

4. As a variation of the above, build a scene in your story by writing the dialogue first. Then go back and add the other elements as needed. (Review Chapter 9 for the elements of a scene.) I frequently use this method when writing my stories. There's a freedom in being able to concentrate only on what the characters are saying and not having to worry about what they are doing or what their expressions and thoughts are.

Notes

CHAPTER 11
The Functions of Narration

*I*n Chapter 9, I stated that there are two ways to tell your story: with scenes and with narration. Chapters 9 and 10 deal with writing scenes. Now we will discuss the role of narration in the story.

NARRATION TO CHARACTERIZE

As we have seen, showing us a person's character is more effective than telling us what he is like. Showing makes him more believable. Showing also makes more interesting reading than telling does. However, there are some situations in which telling may be appropriate.

1. Sometimes it is effective to foreshadow a character's appearance in the story by telling us something about him. In the opening chapter of *Yesterday's Promises*, Andrea almost has a head-on collision while driving home one evening. She believes the driver of the other car to be her brother, Edward, and thinks:

> *She'd have to speak to [Edward] about his reckless driving. Ever since Dad's death, Edward had been a problem. He was twenty-two, two years younger than she, but his maturity had hardly increased since he was fourteen. (p. 13)*

When Edward appears in the next chapter, his speech and actions reinforce what we have been told about him. If you use this technique, be sure that subsequent scenes in which the character participates support and enlarge on what you have narrated earlier.

2. Telling can be an effective means of characterizing minor characters who aren't frequently on scene. Here's another example from *Yesterday's Promises*:

> *Then the door opened and a noisy group of people entered, led by Mayor Hildebrand. . . . On his arm was his wife, whom Andrea had always considered a rather cold woman. (p. 64)*

This information about Mrs. Hildebrand adds to the portrayal of the mayor and his family as more negative than positive characters, which is important to the plot. Remember, don't tell us something about a minor character that isn't purposeful.

NARRATION TO DESCRIBE SETTING

In Chapter 7, you saw how stories may be opened with details of setting, written either objectively or subjectively. You can use these same ways throughout the story to describe new settings. Remember, though, that when you stop to describe something, the action stops. Allowing these narrative passages to become too long creates an "expository lump." A better way to work in many details of setting is to have the character describe them as she moves through the scene, thus combining narration and action. Here's an example from *Yesterday's Promises*. The first is an early draft of the scene with an expository lump of description, and the second is the finished version, in which Andrea describes the setting as she moves through it:

Before:

> *Leaving the museum, Andrea drove north along the Sound for several miles until she reached the Bayport Golf and Country Club. At the gate the uniformed guard gave her a nod and a salute. The road was tree-shaded and winding, and the well-kept golf course was full of golfers, caddies, and motor-driven carts.*
>
> *The clubhouse, resembling a turn-of-the-century mansion, faced the Sound. On warm summer days members enjoyed the private beach. Anyone who didn't care for saltwater bathing could take a dip in the outdoor pool. Nearby were half a dozen tennis courts. For the winter months or inclement weather, these facilities were duplicated indoors. Also inside were racquetball and squash courts, exercise and massage rooms, a cocktail lounge and a restaurant.*
>
> *In the women's locker room, Andrea changed into the one-piece bathing suit she kept in her locker. . . .*

After:

> *Leaving the museum, [Andrea] drove north along the Sound for several miles until she reached the Bayport Golf and Country Club. At the gate the guard gave her a nod and a salute. She continued along the winding, tree-shaded road. On either side stretched the golf course, perfectly groomed, not an off-color patch of grass visible anywhere. Scattered about the course were brightly clad golfers, caddies, and motor-driven carts with colorful canvas roofs.*
>
> *The Victorian-style clubhouse faced the Sound. Andrea parked in the lot overlooking the private beach. The pool*

was empty, she noticed, but it was early in the year for outdoor swimming. There were some players on the nearby tennis courts, however. She watched them long enough to determine that Edward was not among them.

Inside the club, she waved to the young man who operated the sporting goods store just off the lobby. Continuing down the hall, she passed the racquetball and squash courts, from which came the sharp thwacks of racquets hitting balls. She peeked into the restaurant and cocktail lounge, but didn't see any of her special friends. Perhaps she would stop in later, anyway.

In the women's locker room, Andrea changed into the one-piece bathing suit she kept in her locker. . . . (p. 32)

NARRATION OF FACTS NEEDED TO UNDERSTAND THE STORY

No matter where you begin your story, there will be some things that have occurred beforehand that your reader needs to know. Background information about the characters, a situation that resulted in the current problem, or other facts important to the story. To include these things, you must stop the current action and narrate. In the following opening from *A Love Song For Lani*, the sentence in bold italics is an example of narrated information needed to understand the story.

Lani Lorimer stood in the middle of Seattle's historic Pioneer Square, searching for a nightclub called Juliette's. Finally she spied it, an attractive, old brick building on the opposite corner. She crossed the street and when she reached the club paused under the neon sign to check her watch. Five minutes to one. She was early. She took a deep breath, hoping to still the butterflies in her stomach. **This was an important occasion—an audition for a job as singer with the Adam Young Quartet, one of the most prestigious jazz groups in town.**

At exactly one o'clock Lani opened the stained-glass door and stepped into the club's foyer. . . . (p. 1)

In the opening of *Yesterday's Promises*, I included a narrated flashback, breaking it up with a bit of dialogue:

Andrea Kenworth climbed the steps of the Bayport City Hall with less than her usual confidence. As chairwoman of the Concerned Citizens Committee, she had attended many City Council meetings without a qualm, but tonight was different. Tonight an outsider, a stranger, would be present, a certain J. B. Winthrop who wanted to build a large condominium in downtown Bayport. It was the committee's job to stop him.

Andrea had taken over leadership of the Concerned Citizens Committee from her father, Andrew Kenworth, who had died two years ago. "We can't let developers ruin Bayport!" he had maintained, and she had promised to carry on his work.

Now, however, Andrea had some misgivings about her ability to keep her promise. She had lived all her life in this small Washington State community. Could she hold her ground against the powerful and worldly J. B. Winthrop?

In the meeting room, Andrea looked around for her committee. . . . (p. 1)

The danger with this kind of narration is that you may be carried away and allow it to take over the story. You forget about the present and become immersed in the past. Keep the scene moving by working in the narrative parts bit by bit as you go along.

NARRATION TO SUMMARIZE THE PASSAGE OF TIME

On Tuesday Mary meets Dale. Two days pass before she sees him again. If nothing significant happens during those two days, don't go into detail about them. Use narration to bridge the time gap from Tuesday to Friday:

On Wednesday Mary went to work as usual. But it was difficult to concentrate on writing grant proposals for her clients when the image of the handsome blond senator kept popping into her mind. On Thursday her boss caught her daydreaming during a staff meeting and sharply reprimanded her.

Then, on Friday, just as she was about to leave for the day, Mary's secretary called her on the intercom. "A Mr. Dale Hammond is on line one," she said.

"I'll talk to him," Mary replied, her heart hammering as she reached for the phone.

NARRATION TO UNDERSCORE THE SIGNIFICANCE OF ACTION

Often things happen in the story that need additional explanation.

A person says one thing but he's thinking the opposite. A particular scene raises questions in a character's mind that he needs to analyze and consider. Or you, the author, want to call something to the reader's attention.

Such narration is most effective when it is filtered through the viewpoint character. Otherwise, it may become "author intrusion," where it sounds as though you are speaking rather than the character. Avoid author intrusion. It jolts the reader from the story world you have created for him and makes him aware of another (your) presence.

One way to handle this underscoring kind of narration is to place it at the end of a scene. Then it also serves as a bridge between segments of action. Here's an example from *A Dream for Julie*. The first day of skiing is over and Julie is on the ski bus:

> *Julie settled back in her seat. Up ahead she could see Ann and Tom, their heads close together, talking. While she was happy for her friend, it was hard not to feel envious. It had been so easy for Ann to get to know Tom. Why couldn't it have been that easy for me with Eric? Julie thought. But she was not going to give up. Not by any means. At least he knew who she was. Well, not by name yet, but still. . . .*
>
> *Name.*
>
> *Abruptly her thoughts shifted to the boy who had repaired her ski. He had called her by name. How had he known it? She didn't remember telling him. Maybe it was just a lucky guess. Oh, well, it didn't matter. Julie had other things to think about. Like how to get Eric Ransom to notice her.*
>
> *She was determined to get to know him. She had a plan, one that would make him more aware of her than ever. (pp. 21-22)*

This narration has several purposes: 1) to emphasize Julie's determination to reach her goal; 2) to underscore the significance of the "boy who had repaired her ski"; and 3) to reveal that Julie has a plan for getting to know Eric.

Another way to handle this type of narration is to weave it in with the action. In the following scene from *Yesterday's Promises*, Jason has just asked Andrea to lunch. He also wants her to give him a tour of the town's historic buildings. She replies:

> *"Mr. Winthrop, I don't think you're really interested in our historic buildings. I think you want to ingratiate yourself with me so that you can undermine anything my committee and*

*I might do to stop your project. Besides, I'm very busy here
at the museum."*

*Jason Winthrop took a step backward, but his blue eyes
danced mischievously. "Darn!" he exclaimed in mock despair.
"I thought I was being so clever about it. Well, how about
lunch, anyway? Surely you take time out to eat?"*

*She had expected to put him on the defensive, but instead
he had turned her accusation into a joke. Nothing seemed
to disturb the man's good humor. But that gave her an idea.
Why couldn't two play the game? Perhaps she could work
his affability to her advantage. Maybe, just maybe, by using
sugar instead of vinegar, she could make him see her point
of view. Then he would find someplace else to build his condominium. It was definitely a long shot, but, she decided,
worth a try.*

"All right," she said through her sweetest smile. . . . (p. 22)

I interrupted their dialogue only because I felt it is important for the
reader to know at this point Andrea's motivation for accepting Jason's
invitation. Be careful with this kind of interjection. Keep it brief and
purposeful. Don't add narration that repeats what the action and
dialogue shows. Let's take the following exchange between John and
Sue as an example:

John said, "I won't be home tonight until late."

*"I'll see you then!" Sue slammed the door behind him. She
was angry, so angry she could hardly control herself.*

Here, the dialogue and action show us what is going on in Sue's mind.
The exclamation mark indicates her speech is emphatic, and her
slamming the door is an angry gesture. Is it necessary, then, to know
her thoughts? No. We don't need to be told if we are shown. Before
getting inside the viewpoint character's head, ask yourself, does what
I am about to tell add something important that the dialogue or action
does not show?

HOW TO ENLIVEN YOUR NARRATIVE PASSAGES

Narrative passages need not be dull reading. Here are some techniques that will keep your readers immersed in the story while you
are feeding them the information they need to know:

1. Use specific details rather than vague generalities. Being specific
creates vivid pictures that enrich the reading experience.

Before:

> *Jeffrey was a man beset by fear. It was a wonder he was able to hold a job at all. His fear also caused him problems at home.*

After:

> *Jeffrey's entire body shook whenever he demonstrated the new computer. After each session with a customer, he'd have to go to the employee's lounge and pull himself together with cigarettes and coffee. That meant he fell behind in his paper work, and he'd end up taking the work home. His wife, Sara, seeing him pour over it every night, would complain that he didn't pay enough attention to her.*

Which example gives you a clearer picture of this character?

2. Use similes and metaphors to enliven narration. A simile compares two dissimilar things using the words *like* or *as*: Her teeth were like pearls. His nose was as red as a strawberry. A metaphor says that one thing *is* another: Her teeth were pearls. His nose was a strawberry.

Before:

> *Mary sat above the river, thinking.*

After:

> *Mary's thoughts flowed through her mind as swiftly as the river below rushed to the ocean.*

When using a simile or metaphor, make sure the comparison is one that would occur naturally to the viewpoint character.

3. Work in sensual detail:

Before:

> *Trudy spent nearly every day that summer at the beach. Some days were almost too hot for her, but she stuck it out.*

After:

> *Trudy spent nearly every day that summer at the beach. Some days the sun prickled her skin painfully, and not even the cool, salt-smelling breeze or an occasional plunge into the roaring surf would relieve the sting. But she stuck it out.*

4. Break up narrative passages with bits of dialogue.

Before:

> *Mary remembered how her brother Sam always tried to tell her what to do. The older she grew, the more it bothered her. Finally, when they were in high school, she told him she could handle her own affairs. But of course he didn't*

want to cooperate.

After:

Mary remembered how her brother Sam always tried to tell her what to do. The older she grew, the more it bothered her. Finally, when they were in high school, she told him, "I'm a big girl now, Sam. I can take care of myself."

"That'll be the day," he said.

TO DO:

1. To determine your present use of narration, take a scene or a chapter from your book and highlight all the bits of narration and narrative passages. Determine the purpose of each. Check to see if your use of narration falls into any particular pattern. That is, do you tend to use long passages in the middle of scenes? If so, condense them or move them to the end of the scene.

2. Study a scene or a chapter from a published romance by one of your favorite writers. In the same way that you analyzed your own work, analyze hers. Be aware of any of her techniques that you could adopt.

3. Using the methods for enlivening narrative passages, rewrite the following:

A. Jonathan was a man who knew what he wanted.

B. Nora was not someone you'd trust your husband alone with.

C. You couldn't ask for anyone more faithful than Mary.

CHAPTER 12
Developing the Love Relationship

*I*n the middle of the story, the love between the hero and the heroine grows deeper and deeper, while their conflicts drive them farther and farther apart. An important expression of their love is their physical involvement, shown in love scenes.

The content of your love scenes depends on what kind of romance you are writing, sweet or sensual. In a sweet romance, the love is not consummated; therefore, love scenes are concluded or interrupted before the lovers are swept away by their passion. In a sensual romance, the relationship is consummated, and usually the two make love at other times in the story as well.

You need plenty of love scenes, whether they include the sexual act or not. Remember, the love relationship is what your reader wants the most to experience.

Just as you need a plethora of such scenes, each scene in itself must be long enough to fully involve the reader. Both interrupted and consummated love scenes may go on for several pages. When writing a love scene, switch your mental camera to slow motion. Focus on what each partner is doing and what the other's response is. As we discussed in the chapter on style, embellish with adjectives and adverbs and use other words that connote sexuality.

Here's an early love scene between Kezia and Bligh from *The Closest Place to Heaven*, a sweet romance by Lynsey Stevens:

> *In those first few seconds, minutes, hours, Kezia could only let his lips caress hers as surprise held her motionless. But then a sudden yearning began to gather momentum deep within her, rising to dictate her reaction. She was kissing him back before she even knew she was and his other hand moved sensuously up her bare arm to rest against her neck, his thumb brushing along the line of her jaw, now finding the sensitive pulse at the base of her throat. She moaned softly, leaning closer, her body demanding a response while her mind spun crazily, not crediting what was happening.*
>
> *Her hands went out to the solidness of his chest, her finger-*

93

> *tips luxuriating in the damp dark curls, registering the acceleration of his heartbeats as his kiss deepened, plundering, igniting a smouldering glow inside her that burst into a shower of sensual sparks.*
>
> *It was pure pleasure, this heady sensation he was creating, and she simply gave herself up to the reeling enjoyment of that unfamiliar pleasure. This was just as she'd imagined being kissed would be. And more. So very much more. Her hands slid upwards to his silky damp shoulders, thrilling to the muscular strength beneath his tanned skin. (p.30)*

Notice the emphasis on what their hands are doing: "his thumb brushing along the line of her jaw," "her hands went out to the solidity of his chest," and "her hands slid upwards to his silky damp shoulders." Notice the embellishment. Not "her hands went out to his chest," but "her hands went out to the solidity of his chest." And, notice the use of words that connote sexuality: "plundering," "smouldering," "sensuously," "silky."

INTERRUPTED LOVE SCENES

While the characters are making love, their hearts are in control. They are preoccupied by their physical and emotional responses. Then something—usually something external—brings the heroine to her "senses"; that is, puts her head back in control.

To prevent the interruption from appearing contrived, choose something meaningful to the character and that relates to the lovers' conflict. Here's how the above love scene between Kezia and Bligh is interrupted:

> *They could have been the only two people on earth as far as Kezia was concerned, two people in a world of their own, the raft adrift in the blue Pacific, the sandy beach, the fringing shore of a deserted tropical atoll. But the beach wasn't deserted. The thought fought its way through the mists of hazy euphoria. They were in full view of everyone and lots of those people on the beach knew her and knew her well. And they knew Shann. . . .*
>
> *This was all wrong. She shouldn't be kissing [Bligh] like this, this stranger. It should be Shann. . . .*
>
> *"No!" The word burst from her as she churned with uncertainty. (p. 31)*

Kezia is totally involved in the kiss, then "the thought [that the beach wasn't deserted] fought its way through the mists of hazy euphoria."

That thought leads to the realization that people might be watching them. People who know Shann, her intended. That, in turn, leads to the thought that she shouldn't be kissing Bligh; she should be kissing Shann. Now fully aware, she shouts, "No!", interrupting the love scene.

Here's a scene from *The Love Match*, another sweet romance. Diana has gone to Alex's house to discuss his research findings that will benefit her video matchmaking business. Of course the inevitable happens, and they find themselves in each other's arms:

> *Joy flooded through her and for a while she thought of nothing but Alex. But then her gaze flicked to the paper and pencil on the table, and she was reminded of his research project. Abruptly, her mood changed. They shouldn't be doing this. Alex was her client; he was dating other women.*
>
> *Diana put a hand against his chest to push him away. "Alex, no." (p. 113)*

Here, the heroine sees something that brings her to her senses. The paper and pencil remind Diana of the business at hand, and that thought puts her head back in control.

In Blair Cameron's *Million-Dollar Lover*, the extent of the lovemaking itself brings a cautionary awareness to Keira:

> *[Mark's] touch caused shockwaves of sensation to explode through her, awakening her short-circuited brain with a start of cold reality.*
>
> *"Too far too fast, the limit will be soon surpassed." Her grandmother's warning came through as clearly as if she were in the room. Keira pulled herself free from his embrace, panting in quick short breaths. (p. 133)*

It doesn't have to be the heroine who stops the lovemaking. Sometimes it's the hero, as in *Rogue's Bargain*, by Cathy Gillen Thacker:

> *[Lindsey] swayed against him, as pliable and vulnerable as a willow in the wind. Never had anything ever felt so right or more glorious. His lips were warm and smooth, his kiss a gentle exploration, a tantalizing balm for her soul. . . . She answered the kiss, moving her whole body closer into the tempestuous embrace. And it was then, when her lips were infinitely responsive, returning pressure for pressure, wildly reciprocating, that he broke off and moved away.*
>
> *"I'm sorry. I shouldn't have done that." His voice was shaky and low. He seemed abruptly filled with recriminations, the majority of which had to do with kissing her. (p. 120)*

Since we are not in Ben's viewpoint, we do not know exactly why he stopped kissing Lindsey. However, we have Lindsey's reflection that "he seemed abruptly filled with recriminations."

As the story progresses, the love scenes increase in intensity. Here's an excerpt from a long scene between Kezia and Bligh later in their story:

> *The torturing timbre of his kisses began to change, the punishment a persuasion, and she was powerless to prevent her lips parting beneath his as tiny shafts of pleasure rose inside her, enveloping her in a firey cocoon of mindless desire. . . . With practised confidence his hands were arousing beyond endurance while the pressure of his thighs imprisoned her with passionate ease. . . . Her body had not surrendered, yielded completely and unconditionally as a tiny voice from somewhere far away told her she was wavering on the brink of no return, that she was fast losing the ability and the inclination to draw a halt to their lovemaking. (pp. 143-4)*

This is quite a different scene from their first encounter!

CONSUMMATED LOVE SCENES

As I stated earlier, a sensuous romance has a consummated love scene as well as other sexually intimate encounters. There is no rule about how many. What is important is that the consummation be a logical result of the development of the relationship. These are not gratuitous or obligatory sex scenes. Nor are they scenes of forced sex. These people are two mature, consenting adults who are deeply in love, and at that particular moment, despite their conflicts, they have chosen to express their love with a physical union.

What kinds of physical interactions can you use? Radical deviations from the norm, such as sadism and masochism, are definitely taboo, but oral sex is acceptable. The important thing is the language. Employ euphemisms, never street words or slang. For example, a man's genitalia may be described as "pulsating manhood," and a woman's as "her feminine place." The sexual act itself is referred to metaphorically, often as a storm or the roaring surf.

Here's the end of a sensual love scene between Georgia and Simon from *Polished With Love*. Keep in mind that this is the end only; the scene began several pages earlier:

> *Relentlessly, he pushed her forward. There was nothing gentle about his rhythmic movements. . . . Georgia responded on an elemental level which she barely recognized. Her breathless gasps blended with his staccato breathing as, inevitably, the storm broke. He held her writhing body still*

as if to savor her abandoned response to his lovemaking.

Finally, satisfied that she had experienced the full measure of her femininity, he took his own satisfaction, collapsing on her throbbing body with a triumphant shout. (p. 163)

Notice how her orgasm is referred to as "the storm broke," and his as "his own satisfaction." Notice also how he makes sure she has been satisfied. Romance heroes are sensitive to a woman's sexual needs.

MAINTAINING THE CONFLICT

Interrupting love scenes is certainly one way to keep the conflict alive. Along with the characters, we are reminded why these two people cannot get together, why they are not suited for each other. As the conflict is kept alive, so is the sexual tension, that yearning brought about by physically unfulfilled love. This tension builds throughout the story until all conflicts are resolved and the way is clear for the lovers to be together.

In a story where the love is consummated, be sure to end or to follow such scenes with something that reminds the characters, as well as the reader, that these two people still have problems, that their conflicts are far from being resolved. For example, in *Polished With Love*, Georgia, who runs a matchmaking service, tries to help Simon improve his approach to women. As we saw above, their involvement leads to lovemaking. In the next scene, Georgia tells Simon he must date someone from her matchmaking service. He reminds her that:

"I've already got someone I'm not courting to practice on. You!" He smiled triumphantly at her.

A low blow. Georgia mentally winced at his reminder of how he saw her. (p. 170)

The earlier love scene brought them together; this reminder of their conflict pulls them apart. Bring the lovers together, only to separate them again by conflict. This vacillation is an important ingredient in developing the middle of the story.

MAINTAINING SEXUAL TENSION

Sexual tension is not something that is present only in love scenes. Ideally it is a part of each encounter between the lovers. You can infuse sexual tension into any scene by having them 1) think about lovemaking, 2) talk about lovemaking, and 3) casually touch each other.

THINKING ABOUT LOVEMAKING

Obviously this technique belongs to the viewpoint character. Here's an example from *Family Affair*, in which Brady and Sara discuss how her friends are trying to find a man for her. Notice how Brady's thoughts are on something else:

> *[Sara said] "They drag home every available male they find. When I don't snap him up, they just go out and look for another one."*
>
> *You dragged [me] home." [Brady's] mild comment wasn't quite a challenge.*
>
> *"Just to get it over with," she said. "I knew they'd pounce on you, and I decided to speed things up."*
>
> *"How?" he asked lazily, watching her expressive face, letting his gaze linger on her tempting lower lip. He wondered if it tasted as sweet as it looked. He'd find out, he promised himself. Soon. (p. 43)*

TALKING ABOUT LOVEMAKING

Talking about sex but not being able to do it can be very provocative, as on this occasion when Brady says to Sara:

> *"I want to feel your sweet, naked body against mine. I want to hold you so close that I can't tell where your body ends and mine begins. I want everything you have to give." (p. 113)*

CASUAL PHYSICAL CONTACT

In still another scene, Brady manages to caress Sara:

> *Returning to the table, [Brady] leaned over Sara, one hand planted on the table beside her elbow, and organized the remaining pictures.*
>
> *"I took these from the same angles so I'd get the best before-and-after effect," he said. Sara nodded, her attention shifting to the warm thumb absently stroking her arm.*
>
> *"I see," she murmured. . . . (p. 138)*

TO DO:

1. Study the love scenes in the published romances you're reading. If it is a sweet romance, what devices does the author use to interrupt the scenes? Are the interruptions logical or contrived? If it is a sensual romance, how many sexually intimate scenes are there? Note particularly the scenes leading up to the consummation. In both kinds of novels, note how the sexual tension is kept alive in scenes that have to do with other aspects of the plot.

2. Write a love scene for your book. Rework it. Can you lengthen it? Look at the nouns. Can you embellish them with phrases or adjectives? Can you embellish your verbs with adverbs? Have you included the viewpoint character's emotional and physical responses? Does your scene show that the heart is first in control, then that the head restores rationality?

3. Go over all your scenes in which the lovers interact. Can you add sexual tension to them by including thinking or talking about lovemaking, or casual physical contact?

Notes

CHAPTER 13
Creating Suspense

$\mathscr{R}$eaders keep turning the pages for one reason: to find out what happens next. Keep this important concept in mind no matter what kind of story you are writing. You must create a narrative so compelling that the reader can't put the book down.

For your romance novel, you began by developing attractive, interesting characters. You gave them significant goals to strive for and strong conflicts to resolve. You've made their love affair believable and exciting. Here are some more devices that will help you keep a firm grip on your reader's attention.

RAISE QUESTIONS

One way to keep a reader interested is to raise questions as the story unfolds. Questions so strong and thought-provoking that the reader must continue reading to discover the answers. Will George get to the train station on time? Can Laura convince her parents she needs that after school job? Was Henry really at the movies on Saturday night?

Don't confuse these kinds of queries with the overall problem the character is trying to resolve. These are little questions that must be answered along the way.

1. The *action* can raise questions. The things your characters do puzzle and intrigue us. Here's the opening of Brooke Hastings' *As Time Goes By* (Silhouette Special Edition, 1986):

> *The letter came as a shock. It wasn't that Sarah hadn't expected problems, just that she hadn't expected them so soon. It had been only two months, after all; she'd barely had time to get her life back together. She'd assumed they would wait to hear from her.*

After reading this we ask, what was in the letter? What happened two months ago? Who are "they"? We must read on to find the answers.

2. The *dialogue* can raise questions. Consider the following:

> *"I hope you'll make this climb with me," Joe said, pulling out the map of Mt. Rainier and spreading it on the table.*
>
> *"It all depends," Martha said.*

"Yes, I know, on the weather. Well, the forecast for next week is good. We won't have any problem with the weather."

"That's not it."

"What then?"

"I'll let you know tomorrow," Martha said.

Presuming you're involved with these characters and the story situation, wouldn't you read on to find out what Martha will tell Joe tomorrow?

3. The *thoughts of the viewpoint character* can create questions. Cathy Gillen Thacker uses this technique in *Rogue's Bargain*. In the beginning, Ben tells his friend and theatrical agent, Wilhelmina, that he's looking for an actress to star in his dinner theater. After he describes the kind of woman he wants, Wilhelmina says:

"Whoa, Ben. . . . Are you looking for an actress or a friend?"

Ben's mouth curled wryly in mute acknowledgement of her teasing. . . . He very much needed [Wilhelmina] to bail him out of the unholy mess he had going for him in Hawaii. That he'd be killing two birds with one stone only added incentive to make his cockeyed plan work, no matter what the obstacles, and of those there currently were plenty. Unfortunately, he was unable to be one hundred percent honest with Wilhelmina. His deceit was a first; it grated against everything he stood for. . . . (p. 5)

Ben has told us he is being deceitful but not the reason for it. We have to read further to find out why. We do, and learn that Wilhelmina introduces Ben to Lindsey. Ben finds her unsuitable, but we still don't know what he's up to. In another scene Ben hints at his dual purpose for wanting a certain kind of woman:

He had . . . important matters on which to concentrate, starting with his business situation, his next machination. For that he needed someone gorgeous and sultry looking, tempestuous, yet maddeningly indifferent to the attentions of the men around her. (pp. 21-22)

Ben sees Lindsey again and changes his mind about her:

Ben heaved an enormous sigh of relief. Maybe everything would work out for him, after all. If he could convince Lindsey Halloran to cooperate and assist him, he knew he'd be able to manage not just the play but his current business problems, as well. (p.29)

On page 38 we finally find out that Ben wants Lindsey to use her wiles to distract a business rival while he attempts to close a deal with a couple both he and the rival are pursuing.

There are three things to keep in mind about the question-raising technique:

1. No matter which method you use—action, dialogue, or viewpoint character's thoughts—the principle is the same: You, the author, through the characters, are withholding important information from the reader. You are telling her just enough to keep her reading. Imagine being fed one tiny spoonful of your favorite dessert. Then another. And another. Each bite just makes you want more!

2. Don't withhold the information for too long, or the reader will get frustrated. There is no set rule for just how long. Practice and an awareness of how others use this technique will help you develop an intuitive sense for knowing when to withhold and when to reveal.

3. When one question is answered, raise another one. In *Rogue's Bargain*, when we finally find out what Ben's ulterior motive is, we now ask, will she or won't she go along with his scheme? The answer to that creates another question, and so on. When there are no more questions to answer, the story is over.

OFFER SURPRISES

We know a romance will have a happy ending, and that's all well and good. Readers enjoy seeing the hero and heroine reach their goals and solve their problems. But because the outcome is known, it's the journey there that is important. So, surprise us.

Surprises are plot complications that are particularly startling and dramatic. We expect a certain event to occur, but instead something else happens, something we never thought of. Let's take a look at the plot outline of a story we're all familiar with, Robert Louis Stevenson's *Treasure Island*: Each surprise is starred:

> Young Jim Hawkins gets a treasure map from one Captain Bones, just before Bones dies.
>
> Jim gives the map to Squire Trelawney and Dr. Livesey, who decide to outfit a ship and search for the treasure. Jim will accompany them as cabin boy.
>
> Squire Trelawney hires one-legged Long John Silver as cook. Jim recalls that Captain Bones told him to beware of a one-legged man.
>
> When they reach the island, Silver and some of his men go ashore.
>
> *Jim smuggles himself along in order to spy on the pirates.

*Jim meets Ben Gunn, who was with the captain who buried the treasure. Gunn has been marooned on the island for three years.

Meanwhile, Livesey and Trelawney and their men go ashore, find the previous captain's stockade, and set up post there.

The pirates and Trelawney's men battle.

*Jim slips away, takes Ben Gunn's boat, rows to the schooner, and sets it adrift. But, caught in the currents, he finds the schooner bearing down on him. Just before his little boat is rammed, he jumps aboard the schooner.

He fights with the one remaining pirate and kills him.

*When he returns to the stockade, he finds his friends have gone and the pirates are in command.

The pirates argue among themselves and one threatens to kill Jim. *Silver saves Jim. (This is surprising because Silver is supposed to be Jim's enemy.)

Under a flag of truce, Dr. Livesey comes to administer to the wounded pirates.

*Much to Jim's mystification, Livesey gives the treasure map to Silver.

*When the pirates follow the map and dig up the treasure, they find the box empty! (Ben Gunn had moved the treasure to another location, prompting Dr. Livesey to give the useless map to Silver and thus set a trap for the pirates.)

Trelawney and his men rescue Jim.

They sail back to England and divide the treasure.

Notice that in this plot most of the surprises are actions taken by the main character, Jim. If a character's action is the surprise, you must of course portray him as the kind of person who would do such a thing. In *Treasure Island*, Jim's actions are believable because he has been shown to be an adventuresome, courageous youth.

Another kind of surprise is the revelation that proves things are not what they seem. The reader, along with a character in the story, is led to believe something is true, only to find out later that it is not true. In my *Home For the Heart*, Elaine glimpses on various occasions a woman at Justin's house. He has said he lives alone. When she questions him about what she has seen, he tells her she must be imagining things. She assumes he is lying and that the woman is a wife he doesn't want people to know about. This makes Elaine distrust Justin and impedes the development of their relationship. At the end of the story, Elaine finds out there is indeed a woman; but she is not Justin's wife, she is his demented sister.

In short stories, these kinds of surprises or revelations often are at the end, so that the story has one main plot twist. But in a novel you can incorporate such occurrences at other places in the narrative. Be aware, however, that having the heroine meet the hero and think he is someone else is regarded as cliché.

TIME-FUSE YOUR STORY

Another way to add suspense to your story is to time-fuse it; that is, to put a time limit on something. For example, Mary and Tom have decided to call it quits. Mary retreats to her mountain cabin and Tom plans a trip to South America. Mary knows that Tom is leaving at nine o'clock Saturday night. During the interim, Mary comes to realize that she cannot survive without Tom after all. She tries all day Saturday to call him, but there is no answer. A storm comes up and the phone goes dead. Mary then gets in her car to drive to the neighbors, but she gets stuck in a snowbank on the way. Suspense builds as we read to find out whether or not Mary reaches Tom before nine o'clock.

TO DO:

1. As you read published stories, be aware of each time a question is raised in your mind. Note where in the story it occurs. Note the method the author uses (action, dialogue, viewpoint character's thoughts). How soon is the question answered? Does the answer raise yet another question?

2. Repeat the above process with your own novel. Determine if you're telling information that could be withheld to create questions. When you do raise questions, which method do you use?

3. Referring to your plot outline, study especially the actions taken by the characters. Do they always respond predictably? Could they at times take actions that are unpredictable yet in character, to give the plot some unusual twists?

Notes

CHAPTER 14
The End

*T*hroughout the middle you have shown the characters vacillating toward and away from their goals and toward and away from each other. You have increased the tension by having them almost succeed only to encounter a worse obstacle than before. All stories must end sometime, however, and now it's time to wrap things up.

You must resolve all the story lines: the subplots, the personal goals, and, of course, the love relationship. Elements to include in the various endings are: the crisis, the black period, the come-to-realize, and the climax. Each ending will not necessarily include all of these parts. More likely, they all will follow different patterns, depending on how they are intertwined with each other. For example, the personal goal might not have a come-to-realize, but instead proceed quickly from crisis to climax, as in *The Love Match*. In this story, Diana's goal is to establish her video matchmaking service nationwide, but many discouragements, not the least of which is a disappointing affair with Alex, lead to a crisis:

> *. . . She had begun to doubt her calling. In spite of all her successes, all the people she had matched and brought happiness to, Diana did not believe that love, the right love, would ever come into her life. And therefore, she felt guilty about preaching something she didn't fully believe in. She wondered, in fact, if she could actually continue operating Love Match. (p. 174)*

This crisis leads to a decision:

> *Turning to Mitzi [her employee], [Diana] studied her thoughtfully for a moment then blurted, "Mitzi, how would you like to be the owner of Love Match? (p. 175)*

But Mitzi agrees only to run the business while Diana takes a vacation. On the day Diana is to leave, Alex appears and the love relationship is resolved. During this scene the personal goal is also brought to a climax when Diana tells Mitzi:

> *". . . there's been a slight change in my plans."*
> *Mitzi's glance flew back and forth from Alex to Diana. A*

huge, knowing grin spread over her face. "Oh, yeah? Well, I think I know what it is, too. Congratulations!" (p. 183)

In *Yesterday's Promises*, Andrea's goal to keep Jason from building his high-rise has no crisis other than a few tense moments during the city council meeting:

The audience waited in hushed silence while the mayor polled each council member. Three members voted against the construction of Fairview Estates and three voted in favor. Only one more vote to go. Andrea felt faint. What if that last vote were yes? (p. 163)

I increased the tension by having the last voter hesitate:

The remaining member to vote was Dalton Hayes, the man who at the previous meeting had urged more study of the issue. He said now, "I've thought over this matter con- siderably, and there are still a few loose ends that need ty- ing up. For instance—"

The mayor interrupted: "I'm sorry, Dalton, the discussion is over. Please cast your vote."

Dalton frowned.

Andrea held her breath.

"All right," Dalton said finally. "I find it necessary to vote no."

Andrea let out her breath in one long sigh. No. He had voted no. That meant Jason would not build his con- dominium. (p. 163)

Andrea has reached her goal. She also loses Jason, however, so of course the story isn't over.

A subplot in *The Love Match* concerns two people Diana has matched, Ben Watson and Emma Riley. Ben is disillusioned because Emma has changed her appearance. When Ben decides the situation can't go on any longer (the crisis) he decides to alter his appearance to let her know how he feels. The climax scene begins when he comes to Love Match to meet with Diana and Emma:

He had a thick head of black hair that swooped unnaturally low over his forehead. His eyes were hidden by huge dark glasses. His outfit was garish: green trousers, a plaid sports jacket, and a purple tie. . . . [Diana] turned to Emma. "Well, what do you think of the new *Ben Watson?"*

"I like the old one better," Emma declared stubbornly. "And I'm not so sure I appreciate the meaning of this, either. Am

I to assume that my new look is as ridiculous as Ben's?"

"No, no, Emma," Ben said quickly. "I, uh, overdid my change to make a point. . . ." (p. 163-4)

A black moment occurs as Emma continues to stir her coffee and utter, "Hmpf." But then she concedes:

"Oh, take off that silly wig and those stupid dark glasses". . . . Although [Emma's] voice was still angry, Diana noticed that she did not withdraw her hand from Ben's. (p. 165)

A few paragraphs later, Diana leaves, "happy with the assurance that things were going to work out between the two." (p. 165)

In this scene, Emma has a come-to-realize that brings about the resolution of the situation between her and Ben. We don't witness the process because Emma is not a viewpoint character. We do see the results, however, when she tells Ben to "take off that silly wig."

While the endings of subplots and personal goals have a variety of possibilities, love relationship endings usually take the same route. I'd like to say "always," but as surely as I do, you or I will find an exception in the next book we read. So, the love relationship *usually* includes a crisis that results in separation, a black period, a come-to-realize, and a climax. Let's follow the endings of two love relationships, those in Joanna Brandon's *Lingering Laughter* (Candlelight Ecstasy, 1986) and in Cathy Gillen Thacker's *Rogue's Bargain*, to see how these elements are incorporated.

THE CRISIS

Throughout *Lingering Laughter* Lauren has complained that Colby's job as policeman demands too much of his time. Colby has claimed that Lauren's involvement with her family demands too much of her time. Things finally come to a head and, although the two have declared their love for each other, on their way home from an evening out, Lauren says, "I won't be 'on call' for you or anyone else" (p. 180). Colby responds:

". . . After you have expended all your energies on rearranging Tish's love life, or counseling Jeanne on how to raise her children, or bullying your parents into taking a vacation they don't want . . . there's nothing left for me. . . ."

He might as well have slapped her. The effect was the same. Looking like a child unjustly accused of cheating on an exam, Lauren bolted from the car, a sob choking her breath.

She had taken a few steps when she heard the car door

slamming shut. And then, tires squealing, Colby backed out
of her driveway and raced down the street as though he were
answering a call for help. Lauren opened the door and rushed
into the house, flinging herself onto the couch with a pained
cry. (p. 180)

In *Rogue's Bargain* the crisis comes when after a period of separation Lindsey attempts to reconcile with Ben during a court case trying him for unfair business practices. But he refuses her, saying, "It's over. It has been for two months. Don't make it any harder on yourself or on me than it already has been." (p. 246)

Later in the scene, after the trial is over and Ben is declared innocent:

He left the courtroom, surrounded by lawyers and
reporters, sparing her only the briefest passing glance. Lindsey
knew then he was right; it really was over between them.

She left the courtroom, tears blurring her eyes. She couldn't
have said for the life of her why she was crying, from relief
that Ben had been found officially innocent or pain at what
she had thrown away by refusing to believe in him when it
counted most. She only knew the tears wouldn't stop. (p. 247)

Note that while it's not explicit, there is decision-making involved here. The characters' dialogue and actions show that they have decided never to see each other again.

Don't cheat on the crisis! Write an exciting, well-developed scene that leaves the reader believing that the relationship really has ended.

THE BLACK PERIOD

How long the black period lasts and what happens during it depends on your story. Unless something important occurs, use narration to telescope at least part of this time. Here's how it's done in *Lingering Laughter*:

In the days that followed, Lauren kept herself too busy to
think, to remember, to regret. Without her work she might
not have been able to endure the pain and heartbreak.

She saw Colby once while she was at the post office, but
he turned away, pretending not to see her. It was then that
she knew, with a chilling certainty, that she had joined the
ranks of former lovers.

Two long, torturous weeks after the night she'd ended it
with Colby, Lauren finally came to terms with her emotions.
Not that she was happy, or even content. Resigned. That was
the word. The pain of missing him had lessened to a dull

*ache, and she pretended, even to herself, that she was on
the mend. (p. 180)*

During the black period, make the reader feel along with the
characters the terrible sense of loss and the agonizing loneliness that
come with separation from one's beloved.

THE COME-TO-REALIZE

The come-to-realize occurs sometime during the black period. It is
an important plot turning point because it paves the way for the climax.
The come-to-realize must not be a sudden awareness you throw in to
manipulate the outcome of the story. It must be prepared for, a logical
outgrowth of the preceding action. Here's what happens to Colby during
his and Lauren's black period. Colby arises one morning and begins
to shave:

> *"Ouch! Damn!" Colby lowered his hand and, for the space
> of a heartbeat, stared at the blood that was oozing from a
> small cut on his chin and flowing down to dampen the collar
> of his pajama top.*
>
> *He'd had a hellish night. One of many. Lauren's memory
> was merciless, strong, determined. Even when he succeeded
> in sleeping, her image floated in and out of his dreams.*
>
> *"You're a damned fool," he told the hollow-eyed reflec-
> tion in the mirror.*
>
> *And unlike Lauren, he couldn't lose himself in his work.
> . . . How she would laugh if she only knew that the job he
> had thought so important had lost its appeal. He realized
> now that she'd been right all along. He had been so obsessed
> with his job he had made her feel unimportant. And no
> woman liked to be taken for granted. It was a wonder Lauren
> had put up with it for as long as she had. He flung down
> his razor with a muttered curse.*
>
> *Turning on his heel . . . he strode across the tiled floor
> . . . in his hurry to get to the phone. (p. 182)*

While the character may come to his senses on his own, as Colby
does, another way to bring about a character's come-to-realize is to
have a minor character participate. In *Rogue's Bargain*, Wilhelmina,
throughout the story Ben's friend and confidant, says to him during
his and Lindsey's black period:

> *"Ben, you and Lindsey had something. You've finally got
> a chance to build something real and meaningful. Don't let
> that chance, or her, slip away. You know you still love her.*

*I'm telling you she still loves you. Go to her. Work this thing
out no matter how long it takes. For heaven's sakes, give
yourself a second chance. . . ."*

*Wilhelmina's words stayed with Ben the rest of the week.
No matter which way he turned or how hard he worked or
what he did, they were there, haunting him, goading him
to go find Lindsey. So finally, on Friday afternoon, he wangled
a VIP pass and went to a taping of her new television show
at the studio soundstage. . . . (p. 249)*

The come-to-realize results in another decision: The character now
decides to seek out the other for the final reuniting.

THE CLIMAX

In the climax scene, the lovers may apologize for wrongs done to
the other. They may promise change or compromise that will resolve
conflicts. Whatever needs to be done to restore peace and harmony,
they do it, and end by declaring their love for each other. When Colby
goes to Lauren, he says:

*"I'm a proud, stubborn man, Lauren. . . . It's never been
easy for me to apologize, to beg for anything, but I'm begging
you now, Laurie. Give me, us, another chance. I give you
my word that I'll do everything in my power to make it a
good life for both of us."(p. 184-5)*

It takes a while for him to convince her, but finally:

*Lauren lifted her radiant face to his, her eyes misty with
happiness. She smiled as his mouth moved downward, and
opened her lips to invite his exploration of her mouth. She
knew he couldn't change overnight, but she was happy just
knowing that he was willing to try.*

*And they were together, which was all that really mattered.
(p. 186)*

And when Ben and Lindsey get together, Ben begins:

*"I know I said before it was too late, and I thought it was,
but Wilhelmina has convinced me . . . that I'm being a jerk,
and after a lot of ruminating on my part, I think she's right.
I love you, Lindsey. . . ." (p. 251)*

They talk things over for a while, and the scene—as well as the
book—ends with:

*"I love you, too." [Lindsey] put her index finger to his lips
in a cautioning manner. "And it's not too late." Linking her*

hands behind his head, she drew his lips down to hers and sealed her declaration with a long, soulful kiss.

Ben returned the embrace with more tenderness than he'd ever known himself to possess. "You're right," he whispered, "for love it's never too late." (p. 252)

THE DENOUEMENT

Once the lovers reunite for the final time, your story is over. If you can, end with that scene. If you still have loose ends to tie up, do so briefly in a denouement. However, try to resolve other plots and subplots before the climax. For example, in *Lingering Laughter* one of the subplots is that Lauren, who operates an answering service, has been receiving obscene phone calls. Before the climax scene she learns that her troubled nephew is the culprit. And in *Rogue's Bargain* the subplot concerning Ben's revenging a man who wronged him is resolved with the court trial which, as we saw, was also part of the crisis in the love relationship.

TO DO:

1. In the published books you're reading, analyze the ends of the various story lines. What elements does each plot ending have? Carefully study the love relationship, beginning with the crisis. How long does the separation last? What happens in the interim? Which character has the come-to-realize? How is the come-to-realize brought about? Is the climax in which the lovers reunite the last scene? Or are loose ends tied up in a denouement?

2. Write your book's ending. Analyze it in the same way you've analyzed the endings of the published romances.

Notes

CHAPTER 15

Rewriting

*C*ongratulations! You've finished the first draft of your romance novel. Perhaps you've been rewriting, editing, and polishing as you went along. There's nothing wrong with that. I usually go over each chapter as soon as it is completed and make corrections and changes that come immediately to mind.

Now that the entire manuscript is done, however, other changes may need to be made. Let's hope things have fallen into place neatly enough that a major rewrite is not necessary. But if you discover after working through this chapter that you need to tear things apart and begin again, don't be discouraged. All professional writers will agree that writing is mostly *rewriting*. Expect to do a certain amount of it.

What follows is my procedure for turning the first draft into the final draft. Perhaps it will not work for you. There are many ways to evaluate a manuscript. Try my method, though, and where it doesn't work adapt it to fit your needs. See the Bibliography for other books to help with this phase of the writing.

THE BIG PICTURE

Begin by thinking about the story as a whole. Summarize the story in a brief paragraph. For example:

Yesterday's Promises tells how Andrea tries to remain loyal to her late father's wish to keep Bayport a small town. But Jason, who wants to build a high-rise there, shows her that a compromise is the best for everyone concerned.

Then break the big picture into smaller and smaller parts.

CHAPTERS

Using your chapter-by-chapter outline, review what happens in the story. Ask these questions:

1. Does something important happen in each chapter, something that moves the story ahead?

2. Is there conflict in each chapter?

3. Are there scenes between the hero and heroine in each chapter?

This is not to say that there must be, but if you see that several chapters have gone by without the hero and heroine interacting, you might want to do some restructuring.

4. Are the other plots and subplots given regular attention? Be careful that a subplot begun early in the story has not disappeared only to surface again near the end of the book. Any story threads that you begin you must continue to develop throughout the book.

5. Note the crisis in the love relationship. Where is it in relation to the climax? What happens in the interim? Does the story lose tension because too much time has elapsed?

6. Do you have a denouement, or does the story end with the lovers reuniting for the last time? If you do have a denouement, make sure it's not too long. Rewrite to tie up more of the loose ends before the climax. Remember, your story is essentially over once the lovers have resolved their conflicts.

Next, read the chapters themselves. Determine the rise and fall of action in each. Note how each ends. Could you make a stronger hook at the end by foreshadowing action to come, by adding an intriguing viewpoint introspection, or by stopping in the middle of an exciting scene?

Without looking at your chapter outline, summarize each chapter after you read it. Include a sentence or two telling how this chapter moves the story ahead.

When you have finished reading the book, check your latest chapter summaries with your earlier chapter-by-chapter outline. This is important because often things we put in an initial outline somehow fail to appear in the story.

SCENES

Study each scene, checking it against the list of scene elements in Chapter 9. Remember, not all the elements will be needed in every scene. Ask:

1. Does the scene have a beginning, a middle, and an end?

2. Does the scene have conflict?

3. If the scene shows a positive aspect of the love relationship, does it include a reminder of the conflict? If not, does a reminder follow shortly afterward?

4. How does the scene move the story ahead? What is the scene's purpose?

5. Does the scene have enough "bits of business": details of setting, action, gestures, thoughts of the viewpoint character? Does it have too many, so that the pace is too slow?

Focus just on the dialogue. Using the list of dialogue functions from Chapter 10, analyze the characters' speeches. Can you make the dialogue do more than it is currently doing?

CONSISTENCY OF CHARACTERIZATION

Follow each character through the entire story, reading only those parts that have to do with him. Check for uniformity of physical description and other aspects of characterization. Does he always have the same color eyes? Hair? Are the traits and tags you have given him displayed often enough to be effective yet not so frequently that they draw undue attention to them?

PARAGRAPHS

Now focus on each paragraph. Do all the sentences belong to that paragraph? Are the paragraphs in logical order? Are some of them too long? In action-oriented books like romances, paragraphs tend to be short.

SENTENCE STRUCTURE

Examine each sentence. Here are some things to look for:

1. The most important idea expressed last. For example, in the sentence "Fred was not honest, although he had some good qualities," the fact that Fred was not honest is the main idea I want the reader to have. The sentence would be better written this way: "Although Fred had some good qualities, he was not honest."

2. Excess words. Cut any unnecessary words from the sentence. "In order to make a good impression, Jack sent Mary a large bouquet of flowers." Omit the superfluous "in order to" and write: "To make a good impression, Jack sent Mary a large bouquet of flowers."

3. Redundancies. Redundancies are needless repetitions of words, phrases, or ideas. "Helen kept thinking over and over that she didn't want Jack to leave her." The phrase "kept thinking" tells us she did it more than once; therefore, omit "over and over" and write: "Helen kept thinking that she didn't want Jack to leave her," or, "Helen thought repeatedly that she didn't want Jack to leave her."

"She knelt on her knees to pick up the scattered pins" contains a redundancy. How else would you kneel but on your knees? Rewrite it this way: "She knelt to pick up the scattered pins."

4. Parallel construction. Parallel construction puts similar ideas into the same kinds of grammatical constructions. If you choose a certain kind of phrase to express one idea, use the same kind of phrase to express other ideas in the same sentence. For example, "Jack told Mary to drive slowly and that she should not put on her bright lights." Express the two directions Jack gave Mary with the same grammatical construction: "Jack told Mary to drive slowly and *to not put on her bright lights.*" Or, "Jack told Mary *that she should drive slowly* and that she should not put on her bright lights."

PUNCTUATION

Quotation Marks

Quotation marks always go *outside* the comma and the period.

Wrong: "I don't know why", Mark said.
Right: "I don't know why," Mark said.

Wrong: He wrote the article "Unfinished Business".
Right: He wrote the article "Unfinished Business."

Quotation marks always go *inside* the semicolon and the colon.

Wrong: He wrote the article "Unfinished Business;" then he gave it to his editor.
Right: He wrote the article "Unfinished Business"; then he gave it to his editor.

Ellipses

The formal function of ellipses (dots) is to indicate an omission from a quoted passage. Let's say you're quoting something someone has written or said, but for whatever reason you don't want to quote all of it. You use dots in place of the parts you've omitted.

1. Three dots indicate an omission within a sentence or a quoted fragment of a sentence:

Spanish, which is the language of Spain, is an easy language to learn.
Spanish . . . is an easy language to learn.

Note that there are spaces between the words and the dots, as well as between the dots themselves.

2. Four dots—a period, followed by three spaced dots—indicate the omission of 1) the last part of the quoted sentence, 2) the first part of the next sentence, 3) the whole sentence or more, or 4) a whole paragraph or more.

Before omissions:

William Shakespeare was born on or about April 23, 1564, in Stratford-on-Avon, England. William's father, John, was a glove merchant. An ambitious man, he married the daughter of a wealthy landowner and worked his way up as a town official. The Shakespeares had eight children in all, but two died in infancy before William's birth.

After omissions:

William Shakespeare was born on or about April 23, 1564, in Stratford-on-Avon, England. William's father, John. . . . married the daughter of a wealthy landowner. . . . The Shakespeares had eight children in all. . . .

Notice that there is no space between the word and the dot that functions as a period. The m in married is not a capital because I omitted the first part of that sentence. However, the T in the word The is a capital because The is the beginning of the original sentence. For more examples, look at the quotes used in this book.

To use ellipses in the narrative passages of your novel, follow the above guidelines. In dialogue, however, ellipses are used somewhat differently:

1. To indicate that the voice or the thoughts trail off:

> *Dan said, "I don't know where he went. . . ."*
>
> *Dan said, "I don't know where . . ."*

In the first example, the first dot is a period, because the thought is complete. In the second example, the thought is not a complete sentence; therefore, it ends with three dots. Note: Editors differ on this point; sometimes an editor will use three dots even if the thought is complete. My advice is to choose one way and stick to it. Let the editor make changes if her policy is different.

2. To indicate hesitation within the speech:

> *"I . . . don't remember."*
>
> *"Did he . . . say anything about me?"*

Don't get carried away with dots and write something like this: "He never knew where Sarah got that idea. . . . ." This will brand you as an amateur. Remember, you will use either three dots or four dots, depending on the circumstances. Never more; never fewer.

The Dash

Like ellipses, in fiction the dash is used either in narrative or in dialogue. It signals an abrupt change or interruption. The interruption is more abrupt than ellipses but not as definite as the period. Like other marks that call special attention to something we say, the dash loses its effect when overused. Here's how the dash is correctly used:

1. To insert a complete sentence:

In Houston—we moved there in May—I made many friends.

Jake—this was the captain's name—was very kind to us.

2. To add a modifier that is exceptionally long or contains commas:

The union leaders—Elroy, McVain, and Thompson—called for a strike vote.

3. To make something stand out for an especially strong effect:

He crossed the finish line—a gold medal winner.

She walked out of the house—forever.

4. To introduce a summarizing statement:

Sarah babysat, cleaned houses, mowed lawns, and ran errands—all this to earn money for college.

5. To show an abrupt break in dialogue (not a trailing off of the voice, as with ellipses):

Dan said, "I don't know where—"
"—To go from here," Tom finished.

WORD CHOICE

Last, look at each word. Yes, each one! Pay particular attention to nouns, verbs, adjectives, and adverbs. Have you used the word properly? Check the dictionary even for words you think you know well. I'm continually surprised at how often a word means something different from what I thought it meant.

You may have to go through this entire process—or whatever procedure you have found that works the best for you—several times before you decide your manuscript is ready to market. If you're like me, you never will be completely satisfied with it. But there comes a time when you must stop and go on to the next step in the book producing process. Say to yourself, this is the best I can do *at this time*. "At this time" will remind you that you expect to grow in your skills with each book you write.

OUTSIDE HELP

Sometimes writers ask friends and relatives for opinions on their manuscripts. Having someone close to you comment on your work can be helpful. Unfortunately, it also can be downright destructive. Be careful! Friends and relatives may want to please you and be only complimentary about what you have written. Or, for whatever reasons, they may say only negative things. Neither assessment will be accurate. Take with a grain of salt the response of anyone you are emotionally involved with.

The same goes for classes or writers' groups where the members analyze each other's works. Sometimes such arrangements can be quite beneficial. But again, be careful. The members of any group will come from a variety of backgrounds, with a variety of skills, levels of awareness, and prejudices. They may not be capable of giving you the kind of help you want, or the help they do give may not be what your manuscript really needs. Don't take anyone's advice about changing your work unless at your gut level you agree with the suggestion. To try to please everyone will result only in your confusion and frustration.

Further, if you find that you always come away from such meetings feeling discouraged and negative, stop going to them! Perhaps this kind of situation is not the best for you.

If you still want another person's opinion, you might try working on a one-to-one basis with a professional you can trust and have good rapport with. By professional I mean someone who has been formally trained as a writing teacher or who is a published writer. This can be costly, but with the appropriate person it can be invaluable. I'd still caution you, however, about working with anyone, professional or not, who gives you more negative than positive feedback. If this is the case, don't continue to work with that person.

But perhaps you are a writer who doesn't want to show your work-in-progress to anyone. That's all right, too. You must decide the appropriate course for you. The important thing is that you get your novel in the best shape you can before submitting it to those in power: the agents and editors who can turn your manuscript into a published book.

Notes

PART III

Marketing
the
Manuscript

CHAPTER 16
Packaging the Product

*Y*our manuscript is finished! It's been reworked, edited, and polished. You've reached the place where you can say, "At this time, this is the best I can do." Now it's time to present the work to an agent or an editor. I'll discuss making that choice in the next chapter. First, I want to deal with the product you will send to whomever you choose.

Notice I said "product." Try to disassociate yourself emotionally from your work. Regard your manuscript as a product to sell. As is true of any product, the package is important. What kind of package should you present to prospective buyers?

The problem in our field is that different buyers require different packaging. Agent A will consider only a query letter; Agent B wants to see sample chapters. Editor C requires the first chapter and an outline not over ten pages; Editor D wants to see only completed manuscripts and no more than a two-page synopsis. Expect to spend some time tailoring your product package to meet the variety of needs you will encounter.

THE QUERY LETTER

Sometimes an editor or an agent requires you to write and ask him if he will review your manuscript. This saves both time and money, in case your story is not something he will be interested in. However, most writers find it difficult to write query letters. How do you condense a 60,000-word manuscript into a paragraph or two and still do the story justice? Admittedly it is difficult, but with practice you will be able to compose a query letter that will get you the desired results. The sample included here is a format that has worked well for me.

In the first paragraph I tell who the main characters are and what their conflict is. If the story has several conflicts, I choose the most important one.

The second paragraph tells the most significant complications. Notice that I do not reveal the outcome of the story. I have omitted it on purpose, to entice the recipient into reading the manuscript.

SAMPLE QUERY LETTER

P.O. Box 238
Edmonds, WA 98020
Date

Ms. Senior Editor
Romance Novels, Ltd.
1103 5th Avenue
New York, NY 10016

Dear Ms. Editor,

Using the pseudonym Hope Goodwin, I have written a 60,000-word romantic suspense novel, YESTERDAY'S PROMISES. Andrea Kenworth is a museum curator in the small town of Bayport, Washington. She has promised her now deceased father that she will carry on his leadership of the Concerned Citizens Committee, a group dedicated to preserving the status quo of Bayport. Jason Winthrop is an out-of-town builder who has optioned a prime piece of Bayport property for a four-story condominium.

Despite their conflict, Andrea and Jason are attracted to each other and spend several romantic interludes together. Their relationship is further complicated by mysterious notes demanding that Andrea disband the committee. Each time she receives a note, something terrible happens: The museum is ransacked; a shed on her property is set afire; and, worst of all, she is left tied up in an abandoned house that is scheduled to be demolished. Who is behind these frightening occurrences? Her brother Edward, who favors expansion? Ray Clark, a citizen who also wants to see the town grow? Or is it Jason? How Andrea keeps her "yesterday's promises" and wins Jason as well make an exciting and romantic story.

Please see the enclosed resume for a list of my published works, which include seven romance novels.

I hope you will want to review YESTERDAY'S PROMISES. Sample chapters or the complete manuscript may be forwarded to you immediately upon request.

Thank you very much. I am enclosing an SASE for your reply and look forward to hearing from you soon.

Sincerely,

Linda Lee

Encl.

The third paragraph says something about me. If your published credits are few, list them in this paragraph, or, if you have a resume, as I do, say that it is enclosed.

Writers often ask, "Should I mention my publications even though they are not romances or other fiction works?" Opinions on this differ; some say list your credits only if they are in the same or a related field; others say mention anything you have published. My advice is that if you have been published at all, say so. If you have authored, say, twenty monographs on the habits of the boll weevil, you needn't list them all, but I do think letting the person know that you are a professional writer is a plus.

Conversely, if you have not published anything, don't say so. Never draw attention to your lack of experience or be apologetic about it. Simply omit this part of the letter.

The fourth paragraph informs the person whether the entire manuscript or only sample chapters are available for review.

I close by thanking the person and adding that I have included an SASE (a self-addressed, stamped envelope) for his reply. Always include an SASE, no matter to whom you are writing; it is a courteous gesture that the recipient will appreciate.

THE PROPOSAL

Some editors and agents want to see first only a part of the manuscript, called a proposal. Definitions vary, but proposal usually means some sample chapters and a synopsis. How many chapters? My preference is not more than fifty pages, which usually comprise three or four chapters. I always choose the first consecutive chapters rather than, say, Chapters 1, 5, and 10. Editors want to see how the story develops from the beginning.

THE SYNOPSIS, OUTLINE, AND SUMMARY

While all these refer to shortened accounts of what happens in the story, opinions differ on exactly what each means. For this discussion, outline refers to a chapter-by-chapter outline, such as the one you used to construct your story. Summary refers to a one- or two-page narrative detailing the story's highlights. Both summary and outline are synopses, in that they tell a condensed version of what happens in the book; therefore, I'll refer to both outline and summary as the synopsis package. (See Appendix 3.)

My synopsis package includes:

1. A list of the characters and a brief description of who they are. This provides a handy reference for the reviewer.

2. A one- or two-page summary of the story. This gives the editor a quick overview of the book. She doesn't have to read the longer outline if at this point the story doesn't interest her. Also, this summary can be lifted out and sent separately to those who want to see only a short synopsis.

3. A chapter-by-chapter outline. I prefer this form because it shows the reviewer the pacing of the book, how the story is actually played out. You may be able to use the chapter-by-chapter outline you have followed to construct the story. But, to make it the most effective selling tool possible, focus on what an editor or an agent will look for in a romance. Here's my list of requirements:

A. Interesting and appealing characters. If you think adding character sketches would help here, by all means, do so.

B. Evidence of conflict. Make sure your lovers' conflicts are clearly defined.

C. An emphasis on the love relationship. Have you included all the highlights of the lovers' interaction? Have you shown the steady progression of their relationship? If their love is consummated, indicate where in the narrative this occurs.

D. Evidence of sustained conflict. Does your outline summarize action that is full of conflict and drama?

E. The crisis. Is it clear that at some point near the end of the story it appears as though the lovers will never resolve their differences?

F. The climax. Does your synopsis show how they reunite for the final time?

G. Have you shown that all the story lines are resolved?

Some writers include bits of dialogue in the synopsis. If that appeals to you, do it. Dialogue not only breaks up the narrative but also helps to show what the characters are like.

ADDITIONAL TIPS

1. Use an acceptable manuscript form. See Appendix 4 for a sample.

2. Always address your manuscript or query to a specific person; never send it addressed only to "Editor." If you do not know the name of the editor, call the publishing house and find out who is responsible for the line you are interested in. The person to whom you address the manuscript may not be the one who ends up reading it, but at least its destination will be determined by someone in authority, rather than by a mailroom employee.

3. Give the agent or editor a reasonable amount of time to respond. What is reasonable? My rule is six to eight weeks. I allow extra time if a holiday has occurred within that period. Then I either write or call the person, not to bug her about getting to my manuscript, but to inquire politely whether she did in fact receive it.

However, even with polite inquiries, sometimes it takes months to receive a response from an agent or an editor. That is to be expected, given the number of manuscripts they receive. I would advise patience, but you will have to decide what your limit is. I do know that if you're working on another manuscript it will make the time seem to go faster.

Notes

CHAPTER 17
Who Will Represent You?

ou now are prepared to submit your project as a completed manuscript, as a proposal, or in a query letter. The next step is to decide if you will represent yourself to editors or if you will have a literary agent represent you. If the editor you want to reach considers only agented manuscripts, then obviously this decision has been made for you. Whatever the situation, you still should understand how an agent operates.

WHAT AN AGENT DOES

An agent's most important job is, of course, to sell your work. For doing so, he receives a commission, a percentage of what you receive. In effect, he owns a portion of your work. Depending on your particular author-agent agreement, he may continue to own a percentage of whatever the property earns, throughout its earning lifetime. For example, if someone buys the movie rights to your story, your agent, whether or not he sold those rights, may own a portion of the money you will receive. Most agents charge either ten or fifteen percent.

The agent sends your manuscript to those editors he thinks will want to buy it. When an editor wants to make an offer on a property, she phones the agent. The agent relays the offer to you and the two of you decide what your response will be. The agent takes your counter offer back to the editor. Negotiations continue until both parties are satisfied and a settlement is reached.

Not all the contract provisions are negotiated at this time, only those Richard Curtis in his book *How To Be Your Own Literary Agent* (Houghton Mifflin, 1984) calls the "deal points." The deal points include the rights the publisher is buying (for example, the right to publish your book in hardcover and paperback); the *territories* in which he will publish the book (the U. S., Canada, England, etc.); how much money he will *advance* to you before the book is produced; what the *payout schedule* is; and how much *royalty* per book he will give you.

When the deal points are agreed on, the editor sends the contract to the agent. The agent looks it over and advises you again. Perhaps you will want him to do some additional negotiating. Keep in mind that although the agent will counsel you to the best of his ability, he is not a lawyer. If you feel you need professional legal advice, have an attorney review the contract.

When an agreement is reached, you sign the contract and the agent returns it to the editor. Now you and the editor can communicate. She will want to consult with you about revisions or other aspects of the publishing process in which you can participate.

The publisher sends your advance against royalties to the agent. He deposits your money in a separate, client trust account, deducts his percentage, and forwards the rest to you.

When the contract and the advance have been taken care of, the agent may appear to fade into the background, but he still is very much a part of the scene. He keeps track of the book's progress and should a dispute arise between you and the editor, he acts as liaison.

WHAT AN AGENT DOES NOT DO

While different agents have their own special services, there are some things most agents do not do. For example, don't expect an agent to teach you how to write. Use other professionals, such as freelance editors and writing teachers, to help you polish your work before contacting an agent. This is not to say that an agent might not offer suggestions for revisions or be willing to review your story after you have made changes. Most agents, however, have neither the time nor the inclination to instruct you in how to write; their main business is selling manuscripts.

If you encounter an agent who wants a fee for helping you to write or edit your book, be sure you understand what you are getting for your money. After the work is done will he then market the manuscript? Some authors have been burned by so-called agents who in reality earn their livelihood—or at least part of it—by assisting in the revision process.

Don't expect your literary agent to double as your press agent. Of course it is to his advantage that your book sells well after it is produced, but, again, his main task is to sell manuscripts, not the final product.

DO YOU NEED AN AGENT?

Many successful, high-income producing writers do not use agents. To help determine whether or not you need one, consider the following:

1. Do you enjoy the challenge of selling? Of negotiating? Some people might enjoy these activities but not on their own behalf. You may find self-representation difficult particularly if you have not disassociated yourself emotionally from your work.

2. How much time do you have to devote to the writing business? If you're writing only part-time, you may want to use all your available energy for creating books rather than for selling them. Even if you are a full-time writer, you may want to reserve all your working hours for the writing aspect of the business.

ADVANTAGES OF AGENT REPRESENTATION

1. An agent may be aware of markets you are not aware of. Further, because of his close contact with editors, he may find out about new markets before they are made known to the public.

2. Editors often review agented manuscripts before unsolicited ones; therefore, your book's turn-around time will be shorter.

3. Editors often take the time to tell an agent exactly why they don't want a manuscript, which they rarely do for unsolicited projects. There's nothing more frustrating than having someone reject your book without telling you why.

4. An agent's knowledge and experience can be useful in deciding which contract provisions to accept and which ones to negotiate.

5. Depending on the person, an agent can provide moral support and encouragement.

DISADVANTAGES OF AGENT REPRESENTATION

1. An agent is one more person to deal with, one more person you need to please.

2. How can you be sure the agent's judgment about your manuscript is valid? You might do revisions for him and still not sell the manuscript.

3. An agent costs you money. Why give up part of your book's earnings if you don't have to?

4. Agents have other clients, sometimes as many as one hundred. As part of a large group, you might not get the attention you desire.

HOW TO FIND AN AGENT

Suppose, however, that you have decided to seek agent representation. The question then becomes, "How do I find one?" Better ask, "How do I find the one who is the best for me?" As in other aspects of life, some people work well together while others clash. Your best friend adores her agent, but you might not like him at all.

That is why, when choosing an agent, face to face contact is the best. Meet the person, talk to him, get an impression of him and how he works. Do your personalities seem to mesh? Do you like him? Does he conform to your image of the person you want to represent you?

Where can you meet agents? Most of them reside in New York. For most of us it isn't feasible to take a trip there just to meet agents. Check your own area or areas closer to you than New York. Many successful agents operate from other parts of the country. Local writers groups may be able to help you contact any literary representatives who reside nearby.

Writers' conferences are a good place to meet agents. Other sources are your published writer friends. Ask them who represents them and if they would be willing to recommend you.

If you must choose an agent without meeting him or knowing someone who knows him, there are several sources that list literary agents. See the Bibliography for suggestions.

HOW TO INTEREST AN AGENT

You must sell yourself and your book to an agent in much the same way you would to an editor. Be confident and assertive. Let the person know that you believe in yourself and your work. Your book is well-written. It is entertaining. Of course people will want to read it. Yes, you've studied the various lines and feel your book would be just right for Publisher X.

When meeting an agent in person be prepared to pitch your book with only a few sentences. He won't have the time to listen to a blow-by-blow account of the plot, nor would he want to even if he had the time. Think of the last time someone described a story to you. Didn't you find yourself losing interest after a while? You may want to have memorized a succinct speech, something like: "My book, *Lover's Quest*, is about two people on a treasure hunt in the Andes. They fall in love in the process and find out that the real treasure is their love for each other. It's 60,000 words, and I wrote it with Publisher X in mind."

Be prepared to answer some questions about yourself, such as:

1. Do you have any published works? Some agents will represent only published writers, so this must be dealt with before you can proceed. But an agent also needs to know because he may be able to use your credits to convince an editor to look at your current project.

2. How serious are you about writing? How much time and effort are you willing to put into it? Does writing occupy an important part of your life, or is it something you thought you'd try doing in your spare time? Most agents are looking for serious writers whose careers they can help build. It takes a lot of time and effort to sell manuscripts, particularly those by new, unpublished writers. The agent will want assurance that his time and effort will be worth it in the long run.

QUESTIONS TO ASK AN AGENT

The author-agent relationship is a two-way street, and you are entitled to do some interviewing yourself.

1. Ask him about his background. Many agents have been in other areas of publishing; some have been editors, some have been and may still be writers themselves. However, there is no school that trains people to become agents; virtually anyone can hang out a shingle.

2. Ask him about his commission. Some agents require that you pay them a commission for everything you sell, even if it is sold by another agent or by you.

3. Does he charge a reading fee? If there is a fee, ask what you will receive for the money. Will he give you a written critique? Will he then represent you? I know of no agency where the payment of a reading fee guarantees representation. Sometimes, however, the agent will refund the fee to you when the manuscript is sold.

4. Does he charge any fees? Some agencies charge handling fees or what they call monthly maintenance fees. Again, know exactly what you will receive for your money.

5. How soon does he report on queries? On manuscripts?

6. How many clients does he represent?

7. Does he have a written agreement? Some agents do; others prefer informal, verbal agreements. One agency I know of doesn't issue a written agreement until the book is sold. Some agreements are limited to one manuscript; some cover all your literary properties. Some are renewed every twelve months and others run indefinitely.

8. What kind of feedback will you receive as he markets your manuscript? Will he send you copies of letters from editors? Will you be able to know at any time what publisher is considering your book?

9. How much will you participate in the marketing strategy? Some writers want to have a hand in determining where their work is sent and others want the agent to decide.

10. What are his submission requirements? Some agents will read queries only; others will look at sample chapters and synopses; still others may want to see the completed work.

If you choose to represent yourself, learn the markets, the rules for submission, and follow them. Learn about book contracts and how to do your own negotiating. (See the Bibliography for books that can help you.) Note: Even if you have an agent, you should understand how the publishing business works. You are the one who signs the contract, not the agent.

No matter what route you take, persevere! When I first entered the writing-for-publication business, a pro told me, "Success in writing is one percent talent and ninety-nine percent perseverence." I didn't know whether or not to believe him. But now, after twelve years and many rejections—and also some very rewarding sales—I know his statement is true; therefore, I'm passing it along to you. Sure, you must learn your craft; that's what this book is all about. But you also need to hang in there. Once you get that first manuscript off to an agent or an editor, begin a new story. If, after exhausting every possible market, the first book doesn't sell, put it away for a while. By this time you'll have other books on the market anyway.

Notice I said "put it away" not "throw it away." Don't throw away anything you've written. New markets open up constantly. The right one for your book may be just around the corner. Also, editors change. If an editor who rejected your manuscript is later replaced, send your book to the new person. She might have entirely different likes and dislikes.

In the publishing business, decisions often are made for subjective reasons. Your manuscript may be well-written and meet the publisher's guidelines, but for some personal reason the editor responds negatively to it and therefore does not buy it. I know it's difficult, especially at first, but try not to take rejections personally. Say to yourself, "OK, that person didn't like my book. I'll keep sending it out until I find someone who does like it."

I hope the writing techniques and marketing suggestions in this book help you to write and sell many romance novels. If you have suggestions for future editions, please write to me at Heartsong Press.

Good luck!

CHARACTER BIOGRAPHY

1. VITAL STATISTICS
A. Name.
B. Age.
C. Birthdate.
D. Birthplace.
E. Physical description.

2. BACKGROUND
A. Parents: names, occupations, outlook on life, etc.

B. Character's relationship to parents.

C. Other significant people: siblings, aunts and uncles, friends. What effect did they have on character's development?

D. What kind of childhood did character have? Generally happy? Sad? Did anything significant happen that will affect him/her in later life?

   E. Education.

   F. Special interests.

3. THE PRESENT
   A. What is character doing now?

   B. Place of residence.

   C. Hobbies and pastimes.

   D. Friends and associates.

4. PERSONALITY
   A. Points of view.

   B. Attitudes.

   C. Traits.

   D. Mannerisms.

   E. Speech patterns.

5. What is character's problem/goal/need?

APPENDIX 2
CHARACTER TRAITS

Aggressive	Dishonest	Intolerant	Reliable
Aloof	Disorganized	Introverted	Selfish
Ambitious	Easygoing	Inventive	Sensitive
Analytic	Egotistic	Lazy	Skeptical
Arrogant	Empathetic	Lenient	Slovenly
Assertive	Forgiving	Liberal	Strict
Careless	Generous	Loving	Stubborn
Cheerful	Gloomy	Manipulative	Suspicious
Coarse	Gossipy	Meticulous	Sympathetic
Compassionate	Greedy	Nonconformist	Thoughtful
Complaining	Gullible	Nosy	Tolerant
Compulsive	Helpful	Organized	Undependable
Conformist	Impractical	Overbearing	Unforgiving
Conservative	Independent	Perfectionist	Unpredictable
Critical	Indifferent	Picky	Vindictive
Cynical	Industrious	Practical	Workaholic
Dependable	Insecure	Prim	
Dependent	Insensitive	Refined	

SAMPLE SYNOPSIS

Linda Lee   Approx. 60,000 words
P.O. Box 238
Edmonds, WA 98020
Phone number (optional)

YESTERDAY'S PROMISES

By

Hope Goodwin

(If you use a pseudonym, put it here. Put your legal name in the upper lefthand corner.)

SYNOPSIS

Characters:

Andrea Kenworth - **museum curator**

Jason Winthrop - **builder**

Edward Kenworth - **Andrea's younger brother**

Bertrice Gilmore - **Andrea's friend and coworker**

Ned Santori - **pharmacist; Andrea's sometime boyfriend**

Harold Hildebrand - **mayor of Bayport**

Ray Clark - **grocery store owner**

Setting: Bayport, Washington, a small town near Seattle.
Plot Summary:

Andrea Kenworth has promised to carry on her deceased father's work as chairperson of the Concerned Citizens Committee, a group opposed to the expansion of Bayport. Jason Winthrop is an out-of-town builder who has optioned a prime piece of Bayport property for a four-story condominium.

As Andrea and her committee set out to stop Jason's project, he and she fall in love. Of course she knows there is no possible future for her with a man who represents everything she and her father oppose.

Add to this conflict Jason's friendship with Andrea's younger brother, Edward. Edward is a problem to Andrea. He refuses to work, spending his time drawing what she considers worthless pictures. Further, he sides with the townspeople who favor expansion. Andrea is afraid that he has invested some of the family money in Jason's project. She finds out a certain Far West Investment Company has purchased the old Benson house. She thinks it is another company of Jason's and that he is surreptitiously buying more town land.

Each time it appears that her committee is gaining headway, mysterious events occur: the museum is broken into and a shed on Andrea's property is set on fire. With these happenings come crudely written notes telling her to disband the committee or else. Is Edward responsible? Is it Ray Clark, one of the hostile townspeople? Or could it be Jason?

At last the City Council passes a height restriction ruling that disqualifies Jason's project. He leaves town without even saying good-bye to her. But Andrea's victory is hollow. She and Ned agree to be just friends, and she is now alone.

She receives another warning. Before she can do anything about it, her brother calls. Too drunk to drive, he wants her to come and get him at the old Benson house.

While searching for her brother inside the dark house, Andrea is chloroformed, tied up, and left in a closet. The following day workmen begin tearing down the house. Andrea thinks she will surely die, but, just before the house crumbles away, Jason rescues her. With him are Edward and Mayor Hildebrand.

At home Andrea finds out that the mayor was behind the threatening notes and mysterious occurrences. A heavy gambler, he needed money to pay off his debts. He wanted to develop his own property as well as land he intended to buy with his Far West Investment Company. Edward had invested his money in this bogus outfit, but was not involved in the threats against Andrea. A cohort of the mayor's, posing as Edward, lured Andrea to the old house.

Jason shows Andrea a new plan for his condominium, one that meets the town requirements. Because both are willing to compromise, they are now free to love each other. When Jason asks her to marry him, Andrea eagerly says yes.

Chapter Outline:

Chapter I. At a city council meeting, Andrea meets Jason Winthrop, handsome out-of-town builder. They clash as she voices her committee's concerns about his proposed condominium, but she is attracted to him and feels he is interested in her, too.

Chapter II. The next morning Andrea and her brother Edward argue. She wants him to stop wasting time drawing pictures and take a job at the museum, but he refuses. Further, he doesn't share her goal for Bayport. He wants extra money from his trust fund, for some "investments." Reluctantly she agrees to ask their lawyer for it. She tells Ned, also a committee member, her idea to circulate a petition proposing a building height restriction of thirty-five feet instead of forty-five feet. Such a restriction would disqualify Jason's project.

Jason comes to the museum. Hoping to win him over to her side, she agrees to have lunch with him. Afterward, while exploring the old Benson place, he kisses her.

Chapter III. That afternoon she sees Jason playing tennis with Edward at the country club. She is alarmed that they already seem such good friends. Jason asks her to take a swim with him, but she refuses.

Chapter IV. Andrea receives a note commanding her to disband the Concerned Citizens Committee. She decides to ignore it. While gathering signatures on her petition, she has an angry confrontation with Ray Clark, a grocery store owner who favors town growth.

Chapter V. On a trip to the peninsula to pick up donations for the museum, Andrea encounters Jason, who's having car trouble. While his car is being repaired, they finish her errand and later have dinner. Andrea enjoys herself until she finds out there was nothing wrong with his car after all.

The lawyer agrees to give Edward some money. Jason comes to the museum regularly, to study old pictures. When Andrea tries to see the mayor to tell him about the petitions, she finds he's in Las Vegas.

Chapter VI. Andrea and Ned attend the country club dance. Jason is there with one of the mayor's attractive daughters. Jason entices Andrea to sneak away with him and dance in the garden. She knows her feelings for him are growing. When she returns to the dance, she finds Ned and Ray Clark fighting.

Chapter VII. On the way home Ned explains to Andrea that the fight was over Ray tearing up one of their committee's banners.

The next morning Andrea finds the museum vandalized. In the mess is a note telling her to give up her fight against Jason's project. Edward denies involvement.

Chapter VIII. Jason helps Andrea and Bertrice clean up the museum. Jason invites Andrea to dinner. She says she'll think about it. Andrea finds the mayor out of town again. Ned accuses her of dating Jason. She tries to explain that she is trying to win him over to their side.

She tells Jason she cannot have dinner with him—people are talking about them. The mayor reluctantly agrees to inform the council of the petitions. Andrea learns Edward has invited Jason to dinner at their home.

Chapter IX. Jason comes to dinner. Andrea realizes that Jason does have a favorable influence on her brother. During a time alone Jason tries to convince Andrea to let their relationship develop.

Chapter X. At the city council meeting the members agree that because of the petitions they need more time to study Jason's proposal. Ned tells Andrea his idea for Bayport Pride Days, a celebration to raise money for the town without resorting to building tax revenue. Jason wants Andrea to meet him out of town, but she refuses.

Chapter XI. Andrea meets Jason after all. They hike and have a picnic on the beach. But things sour when he won't tell her what he knows about Edward's investments. That night there's a fire in the shed.

Chapter XII. The fire department extinguishes the fire before it ignites the main house. The next day Andrea receives another threatening note. She decides not to inform the police but to find out on her own who's responsible. She learns that the old Benson place has been bought by a Far West Investment Company, based in Las Vegas, and that her brother is involved. She surmises it's another company of Jason's.

Chapter XIII. Jason and Edward tear down the fire-ruined shed. Edward shows Andrea plans he's made for a new shed. Jason has helped him realize that his talent for drawing can be used to design buildings. Bertrice tells Andrea that Jason is in love with her, but Andrea refuses to believe it.

Chapter XIV. At the Bayport Pride Days celebration, Andrea refuses to sneak off with Jason. The next day at the museum, he tells her that she is wrong about what her father believed, that he was not so against change as she thinks. This upsets her and she wishes he would get out of her life forever.

Chapter XV. At the city council meeting, the council vetoes Jason's project. Andrea expected to feel elated but finds she has mixed feelings instead. Jason leaves town. Edward enrolls in the architectural course at the junior college. Ned and Andrea agree to be just friends.

Andrea receives another threatening letter. Before she can do anything about it, Edward calls her. He's down by the old Benson place, too drunk to drive home. Andrea agrees to go and get him. When she goes into the dark house, she is chloroformed, tied up, and left in a closet.

Chapter XVI. The next day workmen begin tearing down the house. Just when it appears she will die, Jason arrives and rescues her.

Back at home she learns that the mayor was responsible for the threatening notes and mysterious occurrences. A heavy gambler, he needed money to pay his debts. He wanted to develop his property and other land he would buy through the bogus Far West Investment Company. Edward had invested his money in this venture but was not involved in the threats against Andrea. It was a cohort of the mayor who lured her to the Benson place.

Jason shows Andrea the revised plan for his condominium, that now conforms to town requirements. Because they both are willing to compromise, they are now free to love each other. When Jason asks Andrea to marry him, she eagerly says yes.

SAMPLE MANUSCRIPT FORM

Susan Smith   Approx._____words
Street Address
City, State and Zip Code
Telephone number (optional)

                          TITLE IN CAPS

                              By

                  Susan Smith (or Pseudonym)

     Start typing or printing about halfway down the page.
Always double space and use only one side of the paper. Use
white paper and a black ribbon. Do not use erasable bond or
onion skin.

     Perhaps you have a word processing program that can give you
a word count. If not, to estimate word length, either multiply
the number of pages by 250 for pica type size or by 350 for elite
type size. Or count the words on three typical pages and
multiply the average by the number of pages in the manuscript.
Round off the number to the nearest hundred.

     Leave about 1 1/4 inches at the top of the page and about 1
inch on the sides and the bottom. Do not justify the right
margin. To justify means to line up the words evenly, as they
are on the left margin.

     On each page put your last name, a key word from the title,
and the page number.

     Do not put the manuscript in a binder; leave the pages

Smith - Manuscripts   2

loose. You may send the manuscript in a box, but don't count on
having it returned the same way. Boxes often become separated
from manuscripts once they reach an editor's office.

A better way is to use a padded mailer. Protect the book
with tag or cardboard and rubber bands. Be sure to include
return postage and a self-addressed mailing label.

You can send the manuscript First Class, Third Class, or
Fourth Class. Fourth Class takes longer, of course, but it saves
considerable money. I send most of my manuscripts Fourth Class.

Include a self-addressed postcard with a message that says
the editor has received the manuscript. This will alleviate your
worries about the book reaching its destination.

#   #   #

BIBLIOGRAPHY

FOR BACKGROUND

Cawelti, John G. *Adventure, Mystery, and Romance; Formula Stories as Art and Popular Culture.* University of Chicago Press, 1976.

Guiley, Rosemary. *Love Lines: The Romance Reader's Guide to Printed Pleasures.* Facts on File, 1983.

Lewis, C.S. *The Allegory of Love; a Study in Medieval Tradition.* Oxford University Press, 1958.

Mussell, Kay. *Women's Gothic and Romantic Fiction; a Reference Guide.* Greenwood Press, 1981.

Thurston, Carol. *The Romance Revolution; Erotic Novels for Women and the Quest for a New Sexual Identity.* University of Illinois Press, 1987.

FOR RESEARCH

4,000 Names For Your Baby. Dell, 1962. (Or any other similar book.)

Goodman, Linda. *Linda Goodman's Sun Signs.* Bantam, 1971.

Hopke, William E., Ed. *The Encyclopedia of Careers and Vocational Guidance, 6th edition.* J.G. Ferguson Publishing Co., 1984.

Occupational Outlook Handbook. U.S. Dept. of Labor. Yearly.

Vocational Biographies. Sauk Center Minnesota: Vocational Biographies, Inc., 1984.

FOR REWRITING AND EDITING

Cheney, Theodore A. Rees. *Getting the Words Right: How to Revise, Edit & Rewrite.* Writer's Digest Books, 1983.

Leggett, Glenn, et al. *Prentice-Hall Handbook for Writers.* Prentice-Hall, 1970. (Or any other comparable grammar book.)

Ross-Larson, Bruce. *Edit Yourself: A Manual For Everyone Who Works With Words.* W.W. Norton, 1982.

Strunk, Jr., William and E.B. White. *The Elements of Style, Third Edition.* Macmillan, 1979.

THE BUSINESS END

Balkin, Richard. *How to Understand and Negotiate a Book Contract or Magazine Agreement.* Writer's Digest Books, 1985.

Curtis, Richard. *How To Be Your Own Literary Agent.* Houghton Mifflin, 1983.

Goldin, Stephen and Kathleen Sky. *The Business of Being a Writer.* Harper & Row, 1982.

Literary Agents of North America Marketplace. Author/Aid Research Associates International. Yearly.

Writer's Market. Writer's Digest Books. Yearly. (Includes a list of agents.)

FICTION BIBLIOGRAPHY

Anders, Donna Carol. *North to Destiny*. Bantam, 1985.

Baxter, Mary Lynn. *Shared Moments*. Silhouette Desire, 1982.

Brandon, Joanna. *Lingering Laughter*. Dell Candlelight Ecstasy, 1986.

Broadrick, Annette. *Bachelor Father*. Silhouette Desire, 1985.

Cameron, Blair. *Million Dollar Lover*. Dell Candlelight Ecstasy Supreme, 1985.

Chase, Elaine Raco. *Double Occupancy*. Dell Candlelight Ecstasy, 1981.

Goodwin, Hope. *A Dream For Julie*. Berkley, 1985.

———. *Home For the Heart*. Manor Books, 1979.

———. *The Love Match*. Thomas Bouregy, 1985.

———. *A Love Song For Lani*. Thomas Bouregy, 1987.

———. *Yesterday's Promises*. Thomas Bouregy, 1987.

Guest, Judith. *Ordinary People*. Ballantine, 1982.

Hastings, Brooke. *As Time Goes By*. Silhouette Special Edition, 1986.

James, P.D. *Unnatural Causes*. Warner, 1982.

James, Stephanie. *A Passionate Business*. Silhouette Romance, 1981.

Johansen, Iris. *Tempest at Sea*. Loveswept, 1983.

Krentz, Jayne Ann. *True Colors*. Harlequin Temptation, 1986.

Louis, Pat. *Treasure of the Heart*. Harlequin Superromance, 1982.

Macomber, Debbie. *Friends—And Then Some*. Silhouette Romance, 1987.

Myers, Virginia. *Sunlight on Sand*. Harlequin Superromance, 1984.

Rainville, Rita. *Family Affair*. Silhouette Romance, 1986.

Roberts, Nora. *Irish Thoroughbred*. Silhouette Romance, 1981.

Ross, Dana Fuller. *Tennessee*. Bantam, 1986.

Salinger, J.D. *Nine Stories*. Little, Brown & Co., 1953.

Shaw, Linda. *December's Wine*. Silhouette Special Edition, 1982.

Stevens, Lynsey. *The Closest Place to Heaven*. Harlequin Romance, 1983.

Stuart, Diana. *The Shadow Between.* Silhouette Desire, 1986.

Thacker, Cathy Gillen. *Rogue's Bargain.* Harlequin American, 1987.

Williams, Lee. *Almost Heaven.* Second Chance at Love, 1986.

York, Rebecca. *Talons of the Falcon.* Dell, 1986.

INDEX

A

Adjectives, 34-35
Adverbs, 35-36, 81-82
Agents, 131-35
Almost Heaven (Williams), 47
Anders, Donna Carolyn, 50-51
As Time Goes By (Hastings), 101
Author intrusion, 89

B

Bachelor Father (Broadrick), 48
Baxter, Mary Lynn, 47
Black period, 20, 110-11
Brandon, Joanna, 109-12
Broadrick, Annette, 48

C

Cameron, Blair, 55, 57, 95
Careers, 9-10
Chapters, 115-16
Character
   biography, 13-18
   goals, 10-11, 23
   traits, 11
Characters, secondary, 6
   describe hero and heroine, 56
   characterized through
   narration, 85
   in subplots, 25-26
   in the come-to-realize, 111-12
Characterization:
   consistency in, 117
   speech tags, 76-77
   through dialogue, 71-73
   through narration, 85
Chase, Elaine Raco, 35
Chaucer, 43
Cheney, Theodore A. Rees, 31
Cliches, 11, 44, 55, 105

Climax, 21, 112-13
Closest Place to Heaven, The
   (Stevens), 54, 57, 93-94, 96
Come-to-realize, 20-21, 111-12
Conflict, 10-11, 58-60, 68, 97
   in dialogue, 82
Connotation, 33
Contracts, 131-32
Crisis, 20, 109-10
Critiques and critique groups,
   120-21
Curtis, Richard, 131

D

Dash, The, 119-20
December's Wine (Shaw), 38,
   56, 58,
Denotation, 33
Denouement, 21, 113
Dialogue, 71-83
   adverbs in, 36, 81-82
   combined with action, 77-80
   combined with thoughts,
   80-81
   functions of, 71-75
   in narration, 89-90
   in place of action, 72
   in the synopsis, 128
   punctuation in, 81
   speech tags, 76-77
   techniques, 75-82
Double Occupancy (Chase), 35
Dream For Julie, A (Goodwin),
   25-29, 44-45, 78-80, 89

E

Ellipses, 118-19
Expository lump, 86

Notes

Notes